AUSTRIA

I SALZBURG

From a nineteenth-century lithograph after F. Barberini

AUSTRIA

MONK
GIBBON

London
B. T. BATSFORD LTD

To
REGGIE AND DAFFODIL DINGWALL

First Published, 1953

MADE AND PRINTED IN GREAT BRITAIN BY
WILLIAM CLOWES AND SONS, LIMITED, LONDON AND BECCLES
FOR THE PUBLISHERS
B. T. BATSFORD LTD
4 FITZHARDINGE STREET, PORTMAN SQUARE
LONDON, W. I

PREFACE

TRAVEL books are of two kinds, those which we read in order to enjoy vicariously another man's journey, and those which we read to be as well equipped as possible for our own. In this book I have allowed myself occasional excursions into reminiscence, but my main aim has been to stimulate the interests of other travellers, and to give some of them an opportunity perhaps of reviving and even supplementing their own memories. In what we are told is the century of the common man it is as desirable as ever that those who go abroad should be uncommonly well-informed. It is not the pedant who is needed, but the person of lively imagination, of warm sympathies and of a fairly wide if not an immensely profound knowledge. I have tried to bear such a person in mind even though I am aware at the same time that he may be the very first to notice my own deficiencies.

I would like to express my gratitude to all who have helped me in my work; to the Rev. Alexander Camier; to Samuel Carr, with whom the project was first discussed and whose taste and judgment through all stages of production have been such a reassurance; to His Excellency Baron Lothar Wimmer, Austrian Ambassador in London, who has taken a personal interest in it, and to whom I have been continually indebted, as well as to Dr. Johannes Coreth, Councillor of the Embassy, and Drs. Eugene Buresch and Clement Weichs; to the Chancellor of Austria, Dr. Figls, who received me when I was recently in Vienna; to Min. Sekr. Ernst Marboe of the Bundespressedienst, who was known to me already through his admirable Book of Austria; to Sekt. Rat. Dr. Harald Langer-Hansel of the Bundministerium fuer Handel und Wiederaufban; to that most patient individual, Dr. Hans Mukarovsky of the Bundespressedienst, and to Dkfm. Otto Kuhtreiber; to Dr. Karl Gladt of the Bibliotheksrat, to the Director and to Hans Walpach of the Osterreichische Verkehrs-werbung; to Count Corti; to Dr. Sobek; to Hans Piesch and Frau Hrabal; and to a host of other friends in different parts of

Austria. I am indebted also to the Landesverkehrsamt in Klagenfurt, Salzburg, Innsbruck and elsewhere.

Finally I would like to pay my tribute to that remarkable man
Harry Batsford, who, though he did not live to see my book
completed, took the liveliest interest in its inception and in the
early stages of the work. Those who never met him can still meet
him in the pages of *A Batsford Century*, vital, impulsive, a character
that might have walked straight out of Dickens rather than out
of our so often dull "scientific age". He was a connoisseur, but
he was something more than a connoisseur, he was a personality.
There was nothing perfunctory about his approach to an author
or his subject. One's own enthusiasm was echoed instantly. In a
room submerged almost under books and papers he would dive
suddenly to the floor and start groping for a volume which he
thought might be helpful. Or, searching his own well-stored
memory for recollections of some tiny village that he had visited
years before in the Salzkammergut, he would dictate and send
off post-haste his impressions of it with a note suggesting that
they might be useful as a supplement to one's own recollections.
The best publishers have always something of the midwife about
them, and, if he were alive today, I can imagine Harry Batsford
slapping this volume, as it awaited publication on its return from
the binders, with something of that vigour with which the nurse
slaps the newly-born babe to make it draw its first breath.

Dublin   MONK GIBBON

CONTENTS

ACKNOWLEDGMENT

THE Author and Publishers wish to thank the following photographers and institutions whose work is represented in this book:
Austrian State Tourist Department, for figs. 7, 8, 10, 16, 18–20, 29, 31, 33, 36, 37, 40, 41, 43, 44, 58–60, 63, 66, 69, 71, 72, 76, 83, 86, 90, 92 and 93; W. B. Henderson for photographs by the late Anthony Ayscough, for figs. 9, 23, 24, 42, 56, 57, 70, 80 and 81; J. Allan Cash, F.R.P.S., for fig. 88; Gerti Deutsch, for figs. 2, 84, 97 and 98; Alexander Exax, for fig. 32; Fox Photos Ltd., for fig. 89; A. F. Kersting, F.R.P.S., for figs. 12, 17, 39, 47, 48, 50, 53, 67, 75, 78 and 79; Landesfremdenverkehrsamt, Klagenfurt, for figs. 35, 45, 46, 49, 51, 52, 54, 55, 61 and 62; Landesverkehrsamt für Tirol, Innsbruck, for figs. 73, 77, 82, 91 and 94–6; A. J. Lewin, for fig. 87; Literary Services (Mondiale) Ltd., for figs. 11, 65 and 85; Eric S. de Maré, for fig. 5; K. G. Moreman, A.R.P.S., for fig. 74; Paul Popper Ltd., for figs. 4, 38 and 68; Max Puschej, for figs. 6 and 64; Helga Schmidt-Glassner, for figs. 3, 13, 22, 28 and 34; Dr. Franz Stoedtner, for figs. 14, 21 and 30; "Studio One", Dublin, for fig. 15.

They particularly wish to thank the Parker Gallery for the loan of the original print from which the jacket was reproduced, W. T. Spencer & Co. for the loan of the lithograph from which the frontispiece was reproduced and Kenneth A. Lindley who drew the maps.

LIST OF ILLUSTRATIONS

LIST OF ILLUSTRATIONS

LIST OF ILLUSTRATIONS

2   A Tyrolese Wedding at ALPACH near INNSBRUCK

3 VIENNA: A panorama, with the spire of St. Stephen's (*c.* 1407–33; *architects, Peter and Hans von Prachatitz*)

I

Introductory

No country, not even France, has so rich an historical heritage as Austria. It is easy to fall in love with the contemporary scene; in fact almost every tourist who comes to her does so. But it is quite as easy, if not even easier, for a thoughtful traveller to become obsessed by a past which is so splendid and varied that it seems the epitome not of any single race or nation but of a civilisation; which indeed it is. In her high mountain valleys, carpeted with flowers in the fashion of MacWhirter's famous painting, that so much delighted me when I first saw it as a schoolboy, years ago, in the Tate, one can forget history, and be mindful only of the unchanging sequence of the seasons. But even here one has only to turn back towards the village and very soon a wayside shrine, or the steep slatted roof of some quaintly-shaped charnel house, like the one at Metnitz, brings the past back into focus. It was never very far away.

A nation cannot live entirely on its historical memories, but without sense of continuity, without an awareness that humanity buys its experience down the centuries, the minds of men quickly become *déracinés*, the doctrinaire and the revolutionary appear on the scene with their banners, their portraits and all the paraphernalia of mass conversion, and Youth, instead of worshipping a legendary past, prostrates itself before a mythical future. Austria is in no danger of doing this. The sense of the past lies too strongly upon her.

Nevertheless she is aware of the present, hopeful and alert, although she has found herself on the losing side in two world wars, has seen territories which were once part of her vast hegemony hewn from her, and has become a tiny state which might be likened politically to that area of relative calm which is said to exist at the centre of a great hurricane. The spirit of the nation remains courageous. The average Austrian probably

A.—2   17

regrets the loss of Hungary or of Bohemia about as much as the average Englishman regrets the "loss" of India, which is not a great deal. But the amputation of India at a distance is a little different from the amputation of territory which one can see from the Leopoldsburg near Vienna on a clear day, and the various economic complications attendant upon dismemberment are bound to emphasise the sense of loss. The Austrians have seen many things go into the melting-pot in this century besides their own empire. If the nineteenth century was to them, as to other nations, a relatively blissful breathing-space, even then, they were not spared war and the loss of territory. And before that, as the centuries slipped by, they had had to battle now with the East and now with the West; they had seen the enemy at their gates and within their gates, the Turks in the suburbs of Vienna, or Napoleon sleeping in the Palace of Schönbrunn. Such a race must be inoculated in some degree to the vagaries of fortune.

The good Austrian instinctively rejects a mood of defeatism. He has lost his empire but he would like to feel that he has found, or rather that he still possesses, his soul. He still stands for something in Europe; indeed he may stand for the one thing which can save Europe from itself. He stands for sanity, courtesy, moderation, toleration, courage and patience in adversity.

National consciousness for the Austrian has two rallying points, albeit of a quite different order. There is what might be termed the Vienna legend, that legend of gaiety, frivolity, graciousness and the glorification of a Danube which is not now, and never was at any time, I feel inclined to hazard—except in the per-fervid imagination of some poet—very blue. It is the Vienna of musicians, of woods and beer gardens and song; and in a grim world the Austrian imagination recreates it, almost as though it were necessary to his salvation. The other point is stauncher and perhaps more perdurable. It is the spirit of the mountains, the spirit of the Tyrol, of Andreas Hofer, of all that is unsubdued and unsubduable. Though it is mountain virtue, the plain-dwellers are convinced that they have a share in it. They think of them-selves in terms of leather trousers and shoe slappings. They may live far from the mountains, but enough of the mountains has got

18

into their soul to sustain their courage and to make them take pleasure in wearing the costume of the mountains even when they are middle-aged city-dwellers. Just as their Emperor Franz Josef felt himself most an Austrian when he had escaped to the high, clear air of his beloved Bad Ischl, and just as in old photographs he looks unnatural in a bowler but thoroughly himself in a Tyrolese hat, so in the shop windows and on the sidewalks of Vienna to-day one sees displayed the grey felt costumes for everyday wearing. The growing preference for this national costume among all classes since the last war is, I am sure, ideological rather than economic. The green facings make the contemporary citizen, whether man or woman, feel really Austrian. Those who wear them are proud of their country, proud of its buildings, proud of its magnificent scenery, proud of its traditions, and the green coat lapel, or the chamois beard in the hat, is the token of this pride

Are the Austrians aware of their charm and do they trade a little upon it? I do not think so. It goes far deeper than a piece of psychological stock-in-trade. Real charm is the outward visible sign of an inward spiritual grace. It is rooted in character. The Austrian is naturally friendly, naturally gay, naturally hospitable, naturally trustful. Sixteen or seventeen years ago I could go into a shop in Innsbruck, offer them a cheque in payment for goods, and, though they had never seen me before that morning, and though, on my own admission, I was returning to England in a few hours' time, still my cheque would be accepted without question. The French can be suspicious, the Swiss can be dour—though not nearly so dour in my opinion as they are credited with being—but such is the reputation of an Austrian that the obligation of graciousness lies upon him as a form of *noblesse oblige*.

He lives in some measure upon that reputation. In the stalls of the Cambridge Theatre one night in September I encounter that great authority upon ballet, Arnold Haskell. He is just back from his summer holiday. "Where did you go?" "Austria." "What was it like?" "Five weeks of pure heaven." I do not ask him what were the contributory factors to this heaven, but I am fairly certain that scenery, food and Austrian graciousness were three of them. Blended in suitable proportions they created a serenity at once mental, gastronomic and spiritual, and the writer returned to London convinced that there was still at least one paradise on earth.

The country is its own best propaganda. Tourist authorities decided, a few years ago, to advertise Austria by a picture of a girl lying flat on her stomach in a meadow, studying a butterfly on the end of a grass stalk. I am aware, as everyone must be to-day, that girls have become the one display gambit with which a modern advertiser feels absolutely safe. If the atomic bomb ever gets as far as being advertised there can be no doubt whatever that we will see a bathing belle astride it, whose pre-radioactive comeliness will be the sole justification for her appearance there. But a rather colourless girl in a rather colourless patch of grass together with a not very colourful butterfly was the wrong ambassadress for a country that possesses so much beauty and variety. If girls at all, then a whole bevy of them and in the national dress and with a mountain or a meadow to suggest their native background. I have wandered far over Austria but I never yet saw a sprawling girl studying a butterfly. Instead I have seen them kerchiefed and short-kilted working in the fields as hard as any man—and harder, for there was often no man in sight. They swung a scythe, or they raked hay, or they gathered potatoes, or they drove cattle so that it seemed that the life of the farm was quite as much dependent upon them as upon their male contemporaries. Even in the towns and suburbs of towns they were going about their business with the quick confident step of young women who know their own mind and have only a limited time for dreaming. Women in Austria play their full part especially in the life of the farm. As Buschbeck tells us, "A peculiar etiquette is observed with regard to certain kinds of work. The hen-house and the vegetable-garden are the women's domain. A lad must not interfere with the vegetable-garden. He may do the digging but not the planting and picking. If he does, he runs the risk of being called *Mädl-Bua* (of which lassy-lad is the nearest translation)."

One can go to Austria in a mood of carefree indifference to all political, topographical and historical considerations and still be

4　A children's procession at
　　GRINZING, VIENNA

5　Open-air　dancing　in　the
　　Salzkammergut

6   SALZBURG: The Horse Fountain (1695)

M. Bernhard Mandl, sculptor

22

very happy. I have never seen St. Wolfgang at the height of the season, but my brother-in-law assured me that the scene in front of the White Horse Inn in mid-August outbids musical comedy in its own suit. My own memories of that far-famed spot are very pleasant but slightly less effervescent. There must be hundreds of thousands of people whose Austrian holiday is a matter of laughter and jollity, undarkened by historical or geographical musings; by any speculation as to the nature of the Alps, or by the faintest suspicion that the central fold is mainly crystalline rock and the northern and southern fold mainly sedimentary rock. But a little geography is helpful to the tourist and quite a stiff dose of history can stimulate interest considerably. I remain silent on politics, as indeed for the most part do the Austrians themselves. For centuries their regime remained one of the most enduring in Europe; then suddenly it dissolved as it were overnight. So absorbing is their history—a cross-section of the whole transitional process from barbarism to feudalism, to paternal despotism, to constitutional monarchy—that if Macaulay's New Zealander should ever come to me and ask where he can best study the evolution of European civilisation I shall tell him not to bother about the English, who were saved many of the more acute problems by their insular position, nor about the French, who were too volatile for their actions to be taken as typical, but to concentrate on the Austrians, who had all the problems and a few extra of their own, and who weathered most of them for centuries with a success that may seem curious but that is also highly creditable. "Maximilian I, Maria Theresa, Franz Josef," I shall say to him. "Go away and learn all that there is to be learnt about them, and, when you come back to me, you will know quite a lot about Europe."

It is tempting for the more pensive traveller to make his Austria the Austria of a period, the Austria of Maximilian, or the Austria of Maria Theresa, or the Austria of Franz Josef. Each is interesting. Each has lots to offer. I remember once hearing, from an eyewitness, of a well-known writer of travel books—he is still alive—whose delight in the Middle Ages and in mediæval things was so intense that when they showed him a very beautiful, small ancient town in Austria he burst into tears from sheer

23

intensity of feeling. This, from an Englishman, is quite a lot. I can survive anything mediæval, however beautiful. But if I could have Schönbrunn and its eighteenth-century memories to myself for a morning, to wander through the empty rooms of the palace and along those branching garden avenues between their high walls of green, I know that there would be no danger whatever that I would "cast a cold eye" on what I saw, and that, indeed, freed from the observation of strangers, I might even shed tears.

Middle Ages, eighteenth century, nineteenth century—they are all there, in the towns and in the villages, in a culture as pure as any that survives in Europe. The past is almost too imperative. Once having "Franz-Josefed" for several days at Bad Ischl, my conscience suddenly smote me, for it seemed almost a disloyalty to a country I liked so well to be so exclusively absorbed in her past, and so wholly vague and unspeculative about her future. I asked myself at last, "But what is that future? What can that future be?" Thought presently furnished an answer. I told myself, "Her future must be that of another Switzerland. She has her provinces just as the latter country has her cantons. They tell me in Vienna—though not wholly with approval—that government is becoming more decentralised, and that the provinces are taking more and more on themselves. That will do no harm. Switzerland is all the more secure because the cantons resent too much Berne or too much Zürich. And if Austria can weld a political machine on the lines of the Swiss, she could become the pattern of an enlightened nationalism, or even head a Central Europe Federation."

No one has ever reproached the Switzer with being a bad European. And the Austrian has all the qualities which might make a particularly good European, witness his dealing with not one but four armies of occupation after a world war. He did not like it, but it is quite amazing the success with which he managed to lump it. I asked various Austrians at various times how they had managed it and the reply was nearly always the same: "We just don't think about them. For us they are not there." And the amazing thing was that this policy—ostrich, it might seem, rather than Österreichische—of mingled dignity and docility, worked. Most of the evidences of occupation vanished after a time. One saw few uniforms and there were even stories of the soldiers of the least popular of the occupying powers getting up to give their seats to old women in the bus. Though it will not commend itself to irredentists or to political fanatics I will point the moral here by quoting Laotze's saying, "Gentleness is invincible." Yes, in the long run, and even in the face of that reiterated "No", the Austrians found that their native courtesy was taking effect.

Austria's present geographical status of course bears no relation whatever to the past geographical status or to many of the events in her history. Anyone who wants this vividly brought home to them need only study the contents page of *Austria : her Peoples and their Homelands*, a well-illustrated volume by James Baker, published by the Bodley Head in 1913. Among the chapter headings one reads, "Southern and Western Bohemia", "Through Silesia to Moravia", "Galicia and its People", "In the high Tatra Mountains", "Through Lemberg to Bukowina", "Trieste and Istria", "Down the Istrian Coast to Sibenico"—there is hardly a name on this first page that has any place in the Austria we know to-day. That Austria of mingled races and territories is gone for ever.

On the other hand it should be noticed that, racially and in regard to religion, modern Austria is more homogeneous than many countries. It is no longer a racial melting-pot for south-east Europe as it was in the days of its empire. Its only racial minorities in 1934 were about 50,000 Czechs, most of them belonging to the Vienna working class, 30,000 Croats in the Burgenland and 30,000 Slovenes along the south of the Klagenfurt Basin: 97 per cent. spoke German as their mother tongue, 90·5 per cent. were Roman Catholics. Only in Vienna were the Lutherans as much as 6 per cent. of the population.

Austria is definitely an Alpine country. A glance at any map which shows its physical features immediately reveals this. It starts on the border of Switzerland as a relatively narrow strip of Alpine territory which gradually widens as we move eastwards but which is ribbed with mountain ranges right to the very threshold of Vienna. In fact the Wienerwald, though not actually part of the Alps, is a sort of north-eastern spur of the Alpine system, and only a few kilometres separate it from the Alps proper. From Vienna one can see the last limestone cliff of that great mountain range, neither very high nor very striking, little more than a nostalgic reminder, to this city on the banks of the Danube, that she is queen of some of the loveliest and grandest of Alpine scenery.

The Alps are the backbone of Austria. The Eastern Alps consist of three main parallel chains running from west to east, the central granite ridge rising to over 11,000 feet in the Tyrol, Salzburg and Carinthia. Vast glaciers in the past have eroded broad valleys; smaller glaciers and flowing water have carved out terraces in these valleys, and farming is possible even at high altitudes; whereas on the high tableland in the north-west of the provinces of Upper and Lower Austria, which is really an extension of the Bohemian plateau, the soil is poor, the climate harsh, farming is restricted and the forests extensive. The most fertile and the most extensively-farmed districts lie either east of the lower Inn in the wide stretch between the Alps and the Danube, or in the Vienna Basin and the Marchfeld, to the north of the Danube, which were once part of an inland sea that flooded the Great Hungarian Plain. Winters are cold, summers very warm, there are few woods but instead vast ploughlands. Oak and black pine appear and many of the flora hail from Central Asia and regions around the Black Sea. Geographically, as well as historically, we realise that Austria is a Janus facing two ways.

As in so many countries, the central factor in Austria's evolution is a river. The Danube sweeps in a great curve north of Munich in Bavaria and then continues on a line roughly parallel with the Austrian Alps but well clear of them, as if it viewed them with suspicion, although not above receiving the contribution of their northward-flowing streams. Illyrians, Celts, Cimbrians, Teutons, Vandals, Allemanians, Huns, Goths, Slavs and Magyars have wandered through the regions watered by this river, just as they wandered in the foothills of the Alps. The Danube was a highway down which rivercraft, laden with rock-salt, paddled cautiously. The almost prehistoric Amber Road, along which would come the honey-coloured trinkets from the

26

shores of the Baltic on their way to be sold in Rome and Alexandria, ran south from the Vistula and the Oder, through the Moravian Gap and crossed the Danube to make its way, through easy passes in the extreme Eastern Alps, to the northern tip of the Adriatic. Where the road crossed the river, Vienna came into being. Vienna, "one of the great emporia of Europe as well as an important political centre and a focus of civilisation".

The Celts overflowed into what is now Austria about 400 B.C., replacing an earlier Veneto-Illyrian population and occupying the Danube valley and the Eastern Alps about the same time that they invaded Italy. Nearly four centuries later, about 50 B.C., pressure from Teutonic tribes made them begin to withdraw westward. Their relations with the Roman Empire had been on the whole stable and friendly, and now between 15 and 9 B.C. their eclipse saw Rome anxious to extend the frontiers of her Empire as far as the Elbe and the March. Rome never extended her rule beyond the Danube, which became her great line of defence based on Carnuntum (east of Vienna) and Laureacum (Emms); but Augustus' stepson Drusus conquered the eastern part of Switzerland, Vorarlberg, the Tyrol and Bavaria up to the Danube, and around 50 A.D. the country between the province of Rætia and that of Pannonia (including the present Vienna Basin), which had been left under the nominal rule of native princes, became the Roman province of Noricum with its capital at Virunum (near Klagenfurt). Rome brought civilisation. Wheat, grapes, peaches and cherries flourished along the Danube, and at Carnuntum, the harbour of the Danube flotilla, could be found an amphitheatre to hold 8,000, extensive thermal baths much appreciated by the chilled Romans, and even a garrison of Syrian troops, moved hither in 70 A.D. in case of trouble during the siege of Jerusalem, who brought with them the cult of Mithras. In 168 A.D., after more than a century and a half of undisturbed peace (a phrase to make us prick up our ears) the Marcomanni, pressed by peoples further north, began to give trouble, and it took the Emperor Marcus Aurelius ten years to re-establish order. In 180 A.D. this great Stoic, author of that Golden Book from which our minds are still able to draw solace, died at Vindobona, which stood on ground now part of modern

Vienna. The disintegration of the Empire commenced soon after. Between 300 and 400 A.D. Christianity made its appearance on the shores of the Danube, but before the latter date the Vienna Basin had ceased to be part of the Roman Empire, and the Danube line had been finally breached in Pannonia by the Visigoths, the Marcomanni and the Quadi. Civilisation was back into the melting-pot.

The average tourist, unless he is particularly historically minded, will be content to leave it there—overrun by Bayu-varians, Marcomannians, Avars and the terrible Magyar—until in 955 A.D. the Hungarian hordes of horsemen are defeated on the river Lech near Augsburg and in 975 a Franconian lord, Leopold of Babenberg, is appointed margrave by the Emperor. In the same year Carinthia became a duchy, distinct from Bavaria.

The history of Austria thenceforward may be said to be the history of the two dynasties, the Babenberg and the Hapsburg, a history which extends right into our own era. The Babenbergs—though there were exceptions to this rule—tended to support the Emperor in any dispute with the Pope, despite the papal attitude of the many prelates in their south-eastern territories. Hungary had become converted to Christianity, the Danube was a safe traffic line, and from 1100 the crusades and the pilgrimages to Palestine made it a most important one. Relations with Byzantium were fairly close. Three Babenberg dukes married Byzantine princesses. Towards the end of the twelfth century the Babenberg court at Vienna was a centre of knightly poetry. The greatest lyric poet of the German Middle Ages was said to be a Tyrolean by birth and he lived for twenty years at the court of Vienna. Poets in any age stand outside the welter of events, and across the troubled centuries comes the voice of Walther von der Vogelweide as clearly and as freshly as the day when it was first heard:

> There where we twain have sat together
> Under the linden on the wold,
> Canst thou yet plain see where forever
> The flowers are crushed in grassy mould.
> Hard by a forest, in a broad vale, tandaradei!
> Sweetly sang the nightingale. . . .

28

And how we lay there, if one guessed,
Thou gracious Lord, of shame I'd die,
What he dared do, and how he caressed
Knoweth only he and I—
And a little birdielie, tandaradei!
It will surely silent be.*

The lady's faith in the little birdielie has been fully justified. It has remained discreetly silent across the centuries.

Another court singer of this time sang in Austria outside the castle walls of an imprisoned king, but we shall postpone consideration of him until we come to Durnstein. Of the last Babenberg, Friedrich the Quarrelsome, Sassmann writes: "The Prince had the faculty of adding together his illusions and treating the totals as facts, even if they had not the remotest connection with reality." And Ernst Marboe adds: "His reign was marked by a series of romantic experiments which from that time on became an essential part of Austrian history. A dozen times his fantastic warlike expeditions would meet with failure, on another occasion unexpected success would be his lot." In the middle of the thirteenth century, when all Europe was terror-stricken from the threat of half a million Mongols, Duke Frederick, with a few hundred troops, occupied the fortified castles of Western Hungary and held them successfully till the Tartar tide retreated. Such courage endears him to us, as does his patronage of the "Feast of Violets", an annual festivity when the inhabitants of Vienna would stream out from the narrow city streets and the man who found the first violet would place his hat over it and would run to find the Duke and—after due verification —be rewarded with the privilege of choosing the most lovely or the most distinguished maiden of the court as his dancing partner for the ensuant year.

Duke Frederick threw the dice of fortune once too often. He attempted to seize the crown of Hungary and fell fighting against the Magyars at Leitha. He had no heir and his house became extinct, leaving the country for a time to chaos. Quarrelsome he may have been, yet his poet laureate could say that nowhere,

* Translated by Patricia de Fezzo.

between Rhine and Danube, Elbe and Po, were the peasants so happy as in Austria during his reign.

Hapsburg domination is a much longer affair. It extends from 1273 when the princes of the realm elected Count Rudolf of Hapsburg—who owned much property also in Alsace and in what is now Switzerland—to the kingship, thus vastly increasing his prestige and power in his own territories, until 1918 when Charles, the last Emperor, abdicated. It is illustrious to a degree and for all intents and purposes ends with one of the longest reigns in history, that of Franz Josef, who was Emperor from 1848 until his death in 1916.

As a child and schoolboy I entertained a marked prejudice against the Hapsburg dynasty. There was that unfortunate business of the—possibly—purely mythical cap set on the—possibly—purely mythical pole. My blood boiled at the thought that William Tell or anyone else should be asked to abase himself in this fashion before the pride of the haughty Austrian. Equally prejudicial for some reason was the Hapsburg underlip. Once allusion had been made to it and my attention drawn to it in a history-book, it became a kind of obsession with me. It confronted me whenever I looked at a portrait by Vandyke. It was always turning up in unexpected centuries, and making a prince look sulky and ugly, or spoiling a princess who might otherwise have been beautiful. Perhaps I had been made unduly sensitive to this matter of physiognomical dominants because I had been told that the Gibbons had a "bottle nose" (actually the Monk nose from Cheshire—the Gibbons were guiltless) and I had been promised it, "like your uncle George", as a precious family heritage by facetious elders, or by sisters anxious to revenge themselves for imagined injuries. At any rate, I hated the Hapsburg lip, which completed the work which the unfortunate cap episode had begun.

But the Hapsburg lip is not nearly as predominant as I imagined. It attains its zenith in Leopold I, who hurled back the Turks from the gates of Vienna, and on silver coins of Leopold's reign, or on the ivory statuette on horseback which is in the State Museum in Vienna to-day, you can see such an underlip as might easily have been made to serve as a hat rack. It is also to be found in the

7 Peasant costume of the Murtal, in STYRIA

8 A Styrian peasant band from EISENERZ

9 "Sun group" in the Belvedere Gardens

10 A lily pond at Schönbrunn

Schönbrunn Gardens

Spanish Hapsburgs where, justly or unjustly, it seems to have become the symbol of a gloomy obstinacy. But one can look at dozens of Hapsburg portraits and not encounter it at all. Court painters may have been kinder to court princesses than they were justified in being, but I cannot trace it in any of Maria Theresa's numerous progeny. If it exists at all, then it has become merely an agreeable fulness.

In any case the Hapsburgs are capable of living down even such an underlip. They are perhaps the most interesting dynasty Europe has ever possessed. Since we shall encounter them wherever we go in Austria, and since their exploits are better told in relation to some actual topographical context, I shall be content with the merest outline here, a framework into which the reader can fit subsequent encounters. Rudolf of Hapsburg defeated Ottokar of Bohemia, the "Golden King", at Marchfeld in 1278, and henceforward it would be Austria and not Bohemia that would decide the destiny of the Danubian territories. Despite setbacks, despite occasional inter-family disputes, the Hapsburgs went from strength to strength. A series of marriages gave them what a dozen wars might have failed to give. For example, the Burgundian marriage in 1477 of Maximilian I to Maria of Burgundy, the Spanish marriage in 1496 of his son Philip of Hapsburg to Johanna of Castile and Aragon, the Bohemian marriage in 1515 of the grandson, Ferdinand I of Hapsburg, to Anne of Hungary and Bohemia, coupled with that of Louis II of Hungary and Bohemia and Maria of Hapsburg, all brought immense territorial increments, immediately or in time. In three generations the thing was done and Charles V, grandson of the dazzling and talented Maximilian I, inherited Spain, Burgundy and all the Hapsburg possessions, and was elected King in Germany, and, later, crowned Emperor of the Holy Roman Empire at Bologna. What a heritage, for a man who was glad enough to end his days quietly in a monastery. If it is true that Edward VIII as Prince of Wales was once asked what he would most like in the whole world to have, and replied, "One day to myself," his reply is another confirmation that the responsibilities of kingship or even of princedom lie heavy. The crowns of Germany and of the Holy Roman Empire, which since the

33

fourteenth century had tended to become identified, remained with the House of Austria from 1437 until 1806, when Napoleon abolished the Holy Roman Empire after a life of a thousand years. Francis II had seen the blow coming and had assumed the title of Emperor of Austria in 1804 to give the Hapsburg State a clearer status.

Of the great eras in Hapsburg history the first is that of Maximilian I. Before ever his gloomy grandson Charles had begun his attempt to recreate European Catholic unity, an attempt which was doomed to failure, Maximilian had acquired Burgundy by marriage and held it successfully against the French, and had recovered Vienna from Matthias Corvinus, the King of Hungary, who had taken possession of it and of Lower Austria, and who was planning a great Hungarian Empire in south-eastern Europe. The threat from the East was always a very real one. In 1526 the Turks, who had captured Constantinople in 1453, conquered Hungary, and Austria alone stood between them and western Europe. Don John of Austria's defeat of the Turkish fleet at the battle of Lepanto, in 1571, which gave Belloc his fine poem, was only one episode in this long struggle. In 1683 the second siege of Vienna was raised and in 1686 Ofen was liberated after 145 years of Turkish rule. In 1697 Prince Eugene of Savoy gave the Turk his *coup de grâce* at Zenta, and two years later the Treaty of Karlowitz followed. No wonder that Prince Eugene, although a foreigner, is regarded as one of the glories of Austria and that you will find traces of him wherever you go in Vienna.

The eighteenth century in Austria, despite Frederick of Prussia's treacherous attack on Maria Theresa and the loss of Silesia, is one of great cultural splendour. It is as unique in its own way as the era of Louis XIV in France. The Counter-Reformation had established itself. Maximilian II had given a wide measure of tolerance to the Lutheran creed and had even been suspected of wishing to become a Lutheran himself; but Ferdinand I, who in 1542 could only find four priests in the whole diocese of St. Stephen's in Vienna, appealed to Ignatius Loyola to send instructors and in 1551 the first Jesuits arrived in Vienna. In 1578 Lutheran preachers and teachers were expelled from

34

Lower Austria and their adherents had either to recant or emigrate, as very large numbers did. Hard on the Counter-Reformation—indeed as an integral part of its strategy—came the Jesuit Theatre, Baroque, and presently the Rococo. Austria was to see an epoch of architectural splendour which still remains one of her chief glories. Under Maria Theresa and her son Josef II the arts flourished, life was gracious for the rich and not too unpleasant for the poor, and the Empress remains a great and noble figure, despite Casanova's attacks on her for being a prude and a moral tyrant.

Finally we come to the nineteenth century, which begins in war and humiliation at the hands of the French, passes thence to the Biedermeier epoch of comfort and sentiment and some very strange-looking pieces of furniture, and then makes its slow way —not without occasional tribulations but generally speaking on a wave of increasing wealth and industrialisation—towards its successor "the century of the common man", whose chief claim to community of experience looks as though it might be that of community of suffering. Austria's history is humanity's. Children build with their bricks, displaying the most wonderful patience and concentration, and repeating their efforts, until they have balanced even the most precariously-positioned brick in place. Then suddenly they knock it all to the ground. It has fulfilled its function. It has begun to bore them. If in Austria to-day one periodically comes upon the tragic evidence of man's infantile tantrums, there nevertheless remains a magnificent heritage to delight the traveller. The country is beautiful, and, as well, the prism of the past offers every brilliant ray of the historical spectrum. It is time to go in search of it all, alike of the baroque angel above the altar-piece, and of the gentian on the still partly snow-covered Alpine slope.

II

Vienna

IT is said, though I will not vouch for it, that on a fine night in
spring, if the wind favours, you can stand in the heart of
Vienna near the Hofburg, the Imperial Palace of the Hapsburgs, and smell the scent of pines from the mountains fifty miles
away. It may be true. It may be a flight of fervid imagination. But
one thing is true. If Vienna cannot summon the resinous sweetness of those distant pines to our dilated nostrils, it has other
magic, entirely its own, quite as evocative, quite as nostalgic,
with which to work upon the hearts of the devoted.

One might put it this way. Vienna is a distillation of the
centuries. Its supposed symbol in the hearts of its inhabitants is
the Stefansdom (3 and 11). I wonder. The city has many
symbols, and the great church with its single flanking tower,
soaring heavenwards beside its unfinished companion, is only
one of them. Equally symbolic almost is some little iron-roofed
pagoda at a street corner, placed there sixty or seventy or eighty
years ago for the sale of tobacco and still fulfilling its function,
although every scroll, every wreath, every piece of ornamentation on its cast-iron frontage advertises the fact that it belongs to
an epoch which has gone and will never return.

It has been said that if ever a European Federation came into
being Vienna would have the best claim to be its capital, since
nowhere else have the three main streams of European culture—
Mediterranean, Teutonic and Slavonic—encountered one another
and been fused into a unity. The generalisation is as dangerous as
most generalisations, but, if nothing else, it is a useful reminder
that from the time when the Romans turned a Celtic settlement
on the Danube into a fortified frontier garrison, Vienna has been
a melting-pot in which races, policies, ideologies have mingled
and presently been blended. Vienna stands not so much for conflict, of which it has seen plenty, as for the resolution of conflict;
not for destruction but for conservation, in a mood of senti-

11   VIENNA: St. Stephen's Cathedral (1399–1446): the West Front

Wenzel Parler, architect

12   The Main Front (1721–23), and (*below*)

13   The Treppenhaus (*Lucas von Hildebrandt, architect*)

VIENNA: THE UPPER BELVEDERE

mental piety; not for iconoclasm but for the devout cherishing of such relics as unkind time has condescended to leave her.

One should come to Vienna in a mood of childlike wonder and expectation. It may not be possible to arrive quite as picturesquely as Elizabeth of Wittelsbach did when she came there, in 1854, as a sixteen-year-old girl who had quite unintentionally cut her elder sister Nené out and found herself betrothed to and about to marry the handsome young Emperor Franz Josef. Leaving the amicable confusion of the parental home at Possenhofen, bidding a fond farewell to her well-loved dogs and her even better-loved horses, she travelled in charge of her mother first to Munich— where the Austrian poet Vogl, who happened to be in the city, threw a poem into her lap as she passed in the carriage—and then to Straubing on the Danube, where a tiny Bavarian steamer awaited to take her to Linz. There she got a first foretaste of Viennese warm-heartedness and of the welcome that awaited her in Vienna. The Emperor had travelled all night upstream from the capital merely that he might hand her ashore before speeding back to his duties. She would sleep that night at a quaint local inn and next morning would go aboard the boat which would take her to Vienna, a boat over which floated the red and white flag of the Dual Monarchy as well as the imperial gonfalon in black and gold, and which had been completely decked out with flowers; for the Emperor had ordered every rose in Schönbrunn to be cut for this occasion. She boarded it at dawn and down the river they went, past the castle of Dürnstein (32, 34, and 35) where Blondel found his imprisoned king, past Stahremberg and within sight of the Nibelungen country, past the Monastery of Melk and the cherry orchards girding it, through the Wachau with its fields and vineyards, through the winding channel, with its churning waters, of the *Donaustrunden* where the Lorelei Isa combs her locks high upon one shore and the witch Frau Helche spreads her net of weeds from the other, until, towards sundown, the Vienna woods came into view and the flower-decked steamer berthed at Nussdorf, where the Danube Canal separates from the greatly-widened main stream, to flow through the central districts of the city and rejoin it ten miles further on.

"It was roses, roses all the way," she might have said, like the hero of Browning's poem, in the years afterwards, and with quite as bitter anguish in her heart. For Vienna can promise happiness but it cannot guarantee it; not even to an empress, any more than to the small girl who drives out in April in an *einspänner*—a curious little one-horse victoria—with her parents to the Prater, after making her first Communion, each carriage met with along that avenue of chestnut trees containing at least one Easter Communion child, sitting proudly in the best seat, in a vehicle decorated with artificial flowers—provided by the driver if the parents have been too poor to afford real flowers with which to deck it.

Few tourists, I imagine, arrive in Vienna to-day by boat as the auburn-haired princess from Possenhofen did. Nevertheless we have what in her wildest imagination she surely never dreamed of, magic carpets which can translate us through space and in relative disdain of time and take us where we will. I have breakfasted near Wimbledon Common and been in Vienna that same afternoon shortly after three o'clock, having merely had to remember the cryptic letters B.E.A.—British European Airways —as the modern equivalent of Abracadabra. When the timid (that ignoble body of the self-martyred) once overcome their initial aversion to air travel it grows upon them apace, because of its ease and comfort, and, one feels inclined to add, on account of the beauty which it reveals. On the occasion which I have in mind we flew to Zürich, admiring the French landscape 8,000 feet below us, spread out like some delightful toy model on a tray. But it was from Zürich on to Vienna that, flying between two separate layers of cloud, a sea of white cumulus below us, with rigid and toothed edges, and great deep crevasses, far deeper than any glacier crevasse, and with a further cupola of white a couple of thousand feet above us, that I wondered how that cloud-enthusiast Ruskin, or his compeer, the poet Gerard Manley Hopkins, would have reacted to such beauty. I have seen, when flying, mauve shadows, along the edges of the corrugated ridges of a vast sea of white cloud, which were more beautiful even than those wonderful shadows which one sees cast on a landscape which lies blanketed under white snow. When man escapes into the air he escapes into an element which is not alien to him but which reproduces the very beauties which delight him most when he is in contact with earth, and which, moreover, gives them to him often at a time when earth has lost them. I remember how on that same flight the clouds presently parted and I caught a glimpse of a curve in the silver Danube, still relatively narrow, edged and sometimes cleft by white sandbanks, and presently saw, below us but already well behind us, the airstrip at Linz, that town from which the Wittelsbach princess started her voyage on the flower-decked boat.

Rome was not built, and Vienna is not seen, in a day. One has about as much chance of taking it at a gulp as of taking Paris at a gulp. It is easy to list the buildings that one should not miss visiting, but much harder to suggest an intelligent or even intelligible way of setting about seeing them. The truth is—that inconvenient truth from which every tourist shrinks instinctively —that it would take half a lifetime to see and really apprehend Vienna's riches. One could devote months to the Belvedere, months to Schönbrunn, years to the Hofburg; and then, a little grey over the temples, one could begin seriously thinking about the *Wiener Barockpaläste* or about the city's churches. It is useless being too ambitious. It is better to go away with one building, or one park, or one church firmly fixed in our affections, than to be dazed by a chaotic nightmare, a multiple confusion of impressions which will never sort themselves out.

The salient topographical fact to bear in mind in relation to Vienna is that its First District, that is to say the Inner Town, is enclosed by a horseshoe-shaped series of streets which constitute the famous Ringstrasse, three and threequarters of a mile long. Its sections are variously named Burg Ring, Opern Ring, Kärntner Ring, Schubert Ring, etc., and it is based on the Franz Josefs Kai which runs alongside the Danube Canal. The Ringstrasse, instantly recognisable on any map or air photograph, is not an accident. It is there because the Inner Town once *was* Vienna, and the Ring now runs on the site of the *glacis*, a wide belt of meadows just outside the fortifications which were not finally demolished until the middle of the nineteenth century. The *glacis* was built over and converted into parks and the city's custom barrier was moved to the Gürtel, a more distant series of streets roughly concentric with the Ring. Presently the city expanded even further and began to take in little country towns like Grinzing and Neuwaldegg, which even now keep their individuality. But the key to any map of Vienna is the Ring which commemorates the vanished fortifications of the old city, and, moreover, signalises a tremendous burst of architectural activity of rather mixed conception, in the 1860's and 1870's, when the wealth of a still carefree industrialisation happened to be plentiful.

The Ring, however, is not going to help us if we imagine that it localises or points to a concentration of the baroque, for baroque had overflowed far beyond the walls of the Inner Town long before the fortifications were levelled. It may be said that it was the memory of the Turk which had left the latter there so long, despite the demands for their removal and despite the recognition of the fact that they had long ceased to be of any military significance. But the walls had once saved Vienna, not so much in 1529 when the Sultan Soliman the Magnificent withdrew from before the gates—chiefly because of bad weather and mutiny amongst his troops—as in 1683 when the townspeople themselves, with relatively few regular troops, beat back the Turks under Kara Mustapha, until Sobieski, the Polish King, could bring a great combined force to the rescue of the Austrians and overwhelm the terrible invader, with the aid of generals like Charles of Lorraine, Ludwig of Baden and Eugene of Savoy.

The mercurial Viennese kept the walls because, as well as being mercurial, they are instinctively conservative; but the moment the Turk was safely disposed of, and even before Prince Eugene by the capture of the great fortress of Belgrade in 1717 had clinched the matter, their optimism had evinced itself by a burst of creativity which was quite as active outside the walls as within them. The Karlskirche—the Church of St. Charles Borromeo—which has been called "the incomparable symbol of Vienna as it is, or almost is", stood just outside the walls, the fulfilment of a vow made by the Emperor Charles VI during the plague of 1713, and was meant for a more spacious setting than it now actually enjoys (22). Summer palaces for the imperial family and for the nobility were built in what were then the suburbs, and only the fact that baroque architects planned in relation to the landscape, and therefore were highly conscious of the possible contribution of gardens towards the proper appreciation of their work, has saved these buildings from being hedged in and spoilt by later mediocrity, as the Karlskirche to a certain extent is to-day.

Baroque in Vienna is not concentrated in any one locale but is spread over almost all the vast area, as much on the outskirts of the city as in the Inner Town. The Ringstrasse is an historical and topographical signpost to much, but not to the Baroque.

If we are going to proceed historically we should begin our sightseeing with the Stefansdom, taking only a brief glance first at the not very interesting Rupprechtskirche in the Judengasse, which is the oldest church in Vienna and to which documentary reference is made in 1161 at a time when the original romanesque building on the site of the Stefansdom was already in existence, although destined to be partly destroyed by fire in 1285. The Stefansdom occupied a position almost at the apex of what was seventeenth-century Vienna. But when the Babenbergs moved down into the city from their castle on the Leopoldsberg, a wooded hill above the Danube, in 1140, the site of the cathedral was outside the city walls and the city itself was so small that its southern fortifications ran not on the Ring but on the Graben, where lay a ditch or natural moat which had once been the defence of the Roman garrison. The Babenbergs built their castle in what is now the lovely baroque square of Am Hof, a square which like the other much vaster one, the Hoher Markt, which was once the Roman Prætorium, is almost lost now in the crowded confusion of the Inner City, although it was once the germ of the future Vienna.

Of the great Cathedral (11), which is one of the most important Gothic buildings in Europe, Edward Crankshaw has written, "Never in any building can succeeding generations of architects so blandly have ignored the message of their predecessors. The charming romanesque west front with its two round towers and its lovely door turns an unrelenting back on the sweeping gothic nave; the abortive north tower is astonishingly snubbed by a renaissance cupola perfect both in form and irrelevance; the great south tower, achieving its aspiration in a tall, slender spire, stands over the transept with an air of more than semi-detachment from the nineteenth-century roof, like some Italian campanile, only purest gothic. That roof, a monument to nineteenth-century junketing, is beautifully symbolic—a smooth, steep slope of highly glazed tiles of many bright colours done in a herringbone pattern of extreme clarity which is interrupted by a colossal emblem of the double-headed eagle sprawling all over the choir. At first, one seems to remember, one gasps at this apotheosis of lavatory tiling, but later the shock is absorbed, and before long the Stefansdom without its astonishing roof would be no church at all, certainly not the cathedral of Vienna.''

Alas, within seven years of these slightly exaggerated words being written, the Stefansdom *was* next to no church at all, and that steep, amazing roof had crashed in flames. It is said that the retreating Germans were heartless enough to shell the building from the Kahlenberg. But actually shell fire had done little damage until on April 11th, 1945, sparks from nearby buildings set fire to some scaffolding which had been erected round "the abortive north tower", the unfinished *Adler Tower*. This tower was begun in 1450 and completed with a Renaissance spire in 1556. Relatively low, it is a contrast to the soaring southern *Tower of St. Stephen,* which, completed under Hans Puschbaum in 1433, tapers loftily to a point 446 feet above the street, and which, together with the curious steep pent roofs at two levels, makes the building a unique landmark. A few days later the Cathedral was little more than a wretched and empty shell. The 20-ton bell, the *Pummerin*, cast from the metal of Turkish cannons by Achmer in 1711, crashed through the vaulting and was shattered, a fate that had already overtaken the *Halbpummerin* in the north tower; the baroque organ with its ninety stops blazed into quick extinction; and Rollinger's famous carved Gothic choir stalls (1476–86), as well as the Wimpassing Crucifix, which, incomprehensibly, had neither been removed like the stained glass and the Wiener Neustaedter Altar, nor protected like the tomb of the Emperor Friedrich III and Prince Eugene's tomb, suffered a similar fate.

44

But the Cathedral has risen like a phœnix from its own ashes. The Viennese, to whom its south tower is known familiarly as "Steffl", set to work within a few days of the disaster and one of the first things to be recreated, though on a steel skeleton instead of a larchwood one, was the amazing roof, with its glistening tiles and even its double eagle. The romanesque detail on the west façade is still there, to fascinate us, incorporated during the Gothic period when such acts of architectural piety were rare; the late-Gothic sandstone pulpit stands in the nave with the stone portrait of its builder, Master Anton Pilgram, under its stairs; and the *Dienstboten-Madonna*, the so-called Servants' Madonna, one of the most beautiful statues of Our Lady, has escaped the fate which overtook the Wimpassing Crucifix.

Because the city has few romanesque or Gothic survivals its steeply-towered cathedral is not only a symbol but also somewhat of an anachronism. It is pre-Hapsburg, and not a great deal in Vienna is pre-Hapsburg. Even those three early churches clustering round the Hofburg, the Augustinerkirche, the Michaeliskirche and the Minoritenkirche, "a curious, asymmetrical, ugly duckling of a church, a great sombre hunchback of a church", as Crankshaw—who nevertheless loves it well—calls it, with its stubbed hexagonal tower replacing a steeple shot away by the Turks, even these three churches belong to early Hapsburg days.

If the Stefansdom reminds Vienna of her lengthy heritage, the Karlskirche is the real symbol of her architectural glory (22). Like so much else in this city one cannot mention it without starting a dozen hares, all needing lengthy pursuit. Should one preface it by a dissertation on the Counter-Reformation, on the arrival of the Jesuits in 1550 and their banishment in 1773, in which interval they made Austria almost 100 per cent. safe for Catholicism? Or would it be wise to precede it with a note on Hapsburg piety since it was the Emperor Karl VI who in 1713 made a vow to his patron saint Charles Borromeo to build a church and had the inscription set on its gable: "Vota mea reddam conspectu timentium Deum" (My vow is fulfilled in the sight of the God-fearing)? Or should it be made the text for some general observations upon architectural principles, and the wide divergence which separates the aims of its façade from those which inspire von Hildebrandt's Piaristenkirche (Maria Treu Church) (14), although the two buildings were begun in the same year, 1716?

All these are suitable gambits. But I prefer simply to relate it to the man who built it, the man whom we shall encounter now at almost every step wherever we go in Vienna. He is Fischer von Erlach. It is not his first work, and it is not necessarily, though many think so, his greatest; but if everything else which he designed vanished from this planet it would still be his passport to immortality. He had distinguished compeers, but he remains Austria's greatest and most inspired architect.

It has been pointed out again and again that—thanks once more to the Turk—Baroque came to Vienna late, and, arriving late, remained long. There are those who see in baroque a decadent aftermath of the Renaissance; but what may have been tinged with decadence elsewhere became in Austria and Germany a vigorous creative efflorescence which needs no apology to-day and is its own vindication. It is tempting to think, and I have often thought, that German Baroque is the only kind that matters. Other nations successfully exemplify the vices of baroque, whereas if we turn to Austria and Bavaria we must, if we are not utterly blind, presently perceive its virtues.

Fischer von Erlach was born at Graz in 1656. When, at the age of twenty-four and already familiar with Vienna from frequent visits, he crossed the Alps and made his way to Rome, Borromini was already dead and Bernini was to die in the first year of his visit. Baroque had left Rome, was influencing northern Italy, and would presently influence Spain, Portugal, Germany and Austria; but von Erlach as he drew and copied and studied in Rome came under the direct influence not of its aftermath but of the forces which had preceded it, the gravity of Bramante, the Raphael of the high Renaissance, the genius of Michelangelo, and thence to Bernini, Borromini and Cortona. For five years he studied, producing variations on existing baroque themes as well as practising as a mural painter, practice of enormous importance to him in later collaborations with artists, as for

4   The Piaristen (Maria Treu) Church
(1698)

Lucas von Hildebrandt, architect

15   The Franciscan Church (1603-11)

A. Mall and P. Centner, architects

16   Wrought-iron gates to the Upper Belvedere

example with Daniel Gran in the Hofburg Library and the Schwarzenberg Palace.

We are as far from baroque in spirit to-day in our architecture as it could well be possible for one style to be from another. The dominant motive of our architects is function, utility. The dominant motive of the baroque architect was, quite frankly, enchantment. He designed a building as another man might paint a picture (hence the admittedly direct relationship between the cloud-capped towers in the scenery of the Jesuit Theatre and those magnificent theatre interiors built by Bibiena, with certain actual buildings which presently followed them, for in each case the object was the same, visual rapture). To von Erlach, the Great Dome, whatever its dim-lit serviceability— and even that to me seemed highly dubious—would have appeared a monstrosity, a blasphemy, an obscenity. When he designed he was aware of function, but, since space was not a crucial consideration (why worry if the palace at Schönbrunn had 1,440 rooms or, as it actually has, 1,441? Why worry indeed?) for him function and fantasy were not by any means such an ill-matched pair as they might have been. The real danger to baroque was that, like a child who can command anything he wishes, it should succumb to its own capriciousness. This was temptation which took a genius like Erlach or Hildebrandt to repel.

Stand now in front of the Karlskirche and see how an architect's flights of fancy can be embodied. It is said that von Erlach got the most strikingly original feature of his façade, the two huge detached and unsculptured columns which narrate the actions of the saint in the same fashion that Trajan's Column carries its narration, by a glimpse, from the Pincio, of St. Peter's and Trajan's Column as one whole in the light of the evening sun. But the nineteenth-century Viennese critic who was greatly embarrassed one day to stand by the Trajan Column and suddenly discover Fischer von Erlach's inspiration in the adjacency of the Church of Santa Maria di Loreto by Sangallo the Younger is probably nearer the truth.

It does not matter where the inspiration came from, inspiration there must have been, if only the internal inspiration of

4*   49

genius. It is the two huge columns, so insolently high that when we stand back from the church they seem almost as high as the cupola itself, that stress the whole daring of the conception. Indeed daring is one of the key words where baroque is concerned; a madman puts his conceptions on paper, and a builder, or successive generations of builders, respectfully carry them out.

Von Erlach was no madman. The man who designed the University Church, Holy Trinity, and St. John's Hospital in Salzburg, or the Clam-Gallas palace in Prague, was a good deal more than a mere visionary. It is true that his first commission for Vienna—and it did not come to him until 1687—was to carry out a fantasy in Carrara marble for which Burnacini, an Italian architect, had furnished the idea and Rauchmiller the actual design, and that this Holy Trinity Column or Plague Column which you can see in the Graben, and in which von Erlach himself had much to say, with its nine angels being swept heavenwards in the company of many cherubs on a column of clouds topped by the three persons of the Trinity, suggests an aptitude for torturing stone not wholly appropriate to an architect. But baroque must be allowed its excesses as well as its triumphs.

Not every tourist is architecturally-minded, but those who are can pass from splendour to splendour in Vienna. True it is all past splendour, and sometimes splendour fallen on evil days and even a little shabby, but if we have so much as a grain of imagination it will leave us breathless. Take merely the baroque palaces of the great families: they suggest a city in which the nobles should have been kings and even the commoners princes. The interior of these buildings makes the decoration of the most lavish luxury hotel in existence to-day seem trivial and meretricious. We are an age of vulgarians, and to conceive anything like the staircase of the Liechtenstein Stadtpalast or that of the Daun-Kinsky Palast is beyond us. If we did, we would be humiliated by our own handiwork. We could not live up to it. If these great town houses and their relatively near neighbours, the summer residences, the *Gartenpaläste*, belonging to the same families, were built with money belonging to underfed and unhappy serfs—I do not say they were—their justification is of course dubious; but

they will still continue to remind us that a century shared between the Common man and the Common capitalist (neither of
them persons of very great taste) is perhaps best symbolised by
the pre-fab home, constructed at some profit by the one, to be
presently inhabited by the other. The façade of the Starhemberg
Palace, whose architect is not even known, that of the
Dietrichstein-Lobkowitz Palace, which owes its existence to an
Italian architect, Giovanni Pietro Tencala, Fischer von Erlach's
more ornate façade to the Winter Palace for Prince Eugene of
Savoy in the Himmelpfortstrasse, or Hildebrandt's Palast Daun-
Kinsky, both of which are high Baroque, take our breath away
alike by their relative simplicity, sincerity, nobility and sheer
splendour. Or visit the Schwarzenberg Palace, renamed for the
moment International House, and devoting itself to encouraging
contacts, cultural and commercial, between the nations; and,
passing into the Marmorgalerie, stand for a moment abashed by
the sight of what von Erlach and the artist Daniel Gran could
achieve in collaboration. The interior of the building may not be
very pleasing, the lead garden statue of the Rape of a Sabine may
be less effective than when we see it flattered in a photograph;
but this magnificent salon, with its exquisitely graceful, stucco,
oval reliefs, its vast ceiling-painting, its hanging crystal candelabra
and its bronze and gilt candelabra in the corners of the room, is
beyond flattery; it is of a loveliness that flatters mankind, flatters
it in that man should have conceived it in the first place and then
thought himself worthy to make it a background to the pageant
of his life. It is magnificent, as magnificent as the contents of an
Egyptian royal tomb and as worthy of solicitous preservation.

I do not know how the C.M. and the C.C. react to these
things when they see them, if see them they do. I can imagine
Mozart giving them both delight, for music touches the universal
soul. But when it comes to a von Erlach or a Turner even the
self-styled experts shamelessly disagree, and so the rest of us
may well be forgiven our enthusiasms or our allergy. Mr.
Edward Crankshaw is a talented specialist, yet I am going to
confess that my taste runs counter to his in that I think Schönbrunn (18) a much pleasanter and even a much better building
than the Upper Belvedere (12), I am in love with Schönbrunn,

whereas it would not really distress me very greatly to hear one day that an earthquake had engulfed its rival, provided the terraced garden, the magnificent iron gates and above all the orangery in the Lower Belvedere had survived.

I not only disagree with Mr. Crankshaw but I disagree with Casanova. For besides being in love with Schönbrunn I am quite a little in love with that pattern of courage, propriety and self-dedication the Empress Maria Theresa, who was responsible for its completion, who bore sixteen children to an adored but not excessively faithful husband, although she dreaded childbirth, and whose shade meets one at every step almost when one visits the great palace on the outskirts of the city. Casanova must have been intimidated by the enforced virtue of a Vienna from which he rather quickly removed himself. He writes with considerable malice: "Vienna is a beautiful city: in my day, a rich city, and people lived luxuriously, but the bigotry and narrow-mindedness of the empress made life difficult, especially for foreigners. A legion of vile spies, decorated with the high-sounding title of 'Commissioners of Chastity', overran the place; for the sovereign, who lacked the sublime virtue of tolerance, had taken the register of the seven deadly sins into her own hands and had decided that six of them could be overlooked but that the seventh was unforgiveable." And then getting into his stride he proceeds to put into her mouth the following amazing speech. "One can pardon pride," he makes her say, "for it is nearly allied to dignity. Avarice is frightful, but closely resembles economy. Anger reacts on those who give way to it. Gluttony is but daintiness pushed to excess. Envy is a low passion which is never acknowledged. Sloth finds its penalty in *ennui*. But incontinence is a thing apart, a pure heart cannot tolerate it, and I declare open war on it. I know that in Rome much indulgence is shown to this crime, and that every cardinal has his mistress, but at Rome concessions are made to the climate which I have no need to make here, where the bottle and the pipe are the principal pleasures . . ." and so on, and so on, an apocryphal speech if there was ever one.

When I lunched with that talented writer and archivist Count Corti recently in Vienna, he lamented the fact that the

unpublished portions of Casanova's memoirs had perished during
the second world war in the vaults of the firm of Brockhaus in
Leipzig. It was an irreparable loss, he explained to me, not because the unpublished portions were still racier than those that
were published twenty-four years after Casanova's death in 1822,
but because they contained much serious material of great value
to our historical knowledge, all of which the Brockhaus descendants hesitated to publish lest it should reveal how scabrous a
selection their forebears had chosen to make in the first instance!
No one was ever allowed to see the original manuscript for this
same reason, a reason favourable rather than unfavourable to
Casanova, and no one will ever have the chance to see it now.

Casanova's Maria Theresa is largely the invention of his own
fertile imagination, and we need not take it seriously. She is not
the type and pattern of prudery, though she is the type of
maternal virtue. Her solicitude for her own huge family—and
she would not have been a Hapsburg if she had not possessed that
—overflowed into a kindred maternal solicitude for the welfare
of the inhabitants of her vast territories. As a schoolboy I had
only one thing against her, that she should be mixed up with
anything as ill-sounding and recalcitrant to memory as the
Pragmatic Sanction. But very soon Macaulay, in one flashing and
utterly memorable sentence, laid bare the treachery of Frederick
of Prussia at the outset of her Seven Years' War, and made me
the adherent of the betrayed Empress for ever. It is many years
since I last read the words but I can still quote what I imagine is
a fairly reasonable approximation to them: "In order that he
might rob a neighbour whom he had promised to defend, black
men fought each other on the coasts of Coromandel and red men
scalped each other along the banks of the Mississippi" (or "in
the backwoods of Canada"?). I defy anyone to get more history,
more *sæva indignatio* and more moral condemnation into a
couple of lines than is hidden in these lines which must have
stuck in many another schoolboy's memory as well as my own.

She was a great and good woman and her image is still current
coin of the realm in a part of the world where she would surely
have been surprised to meet it. At a luncheon in Dorset one day
I happen to sing her praises, whereupon Elwyn Jones, who has

visited Abyssinia on legal business in days before the House of Commons began to claim his attention, takes out of his pocket a silver thaler with the head of Maria Theresa upon it and tells me that from 1780 onwards the Abyssinians have had minted for them, as far afield even as Birmingham, this silver Austrian thaler. It alone is trusted. "In the remote wilds of Abyssinia black chieftains know every jewel upon her corsage and every hair on her head." I learn that when the Emperor Menelek tried to substitute a different coinage the attempt ignominiously failed. And so now, after 170 years, the head of the Great Empress, with all her titles of Burgundy, etc., imprinted round it, and with the motto "Justitia et clementia" forming the bevelled edge of the coin, still circulates from hand to hand in a country in which she never set foot and where it is highly doubtful whether her thoughts ever strayed.

It would be worth going to Vienna merely to see Schönbrunn alone and pass a succession of days enjoying its splendours and its simplicities (10, 17, 18, 21). For that is the whole point of my approval: Schönbrunn despite its size and despite its splendours has an air of gracious simplicity which in a sense is truly homely. Even where its splendours are concerned it is saved by the most perfect taste. They are congruous. They are never excessive. I am quite happy to forget Fischer von Erlach's original grandiose conception for this rival of Versailles and I am even glad that there was not money in the end to carry it out. Schönbrunn, as finished now, does, on of course a much greater scale, exactly what a Danish or Swedish manor house does; it suggests wealth, but it suggests also the serene and comfortable routine of country life. When I pass through its gate, with its splendidly wrought rococo lattice work, its sphinxes, its obelisks topped by gilt eagles which Napoleon put there and which his connections by marriage, the Hapsburgs, never subsequently removed, I see a vast restful expanse of gravelled courtyard flanked either side by an immense long low wing of buildings painted like the palace itself, which stands facing the gate, a warm, friendly "Maria Theresa yellow" (a colour which others may detest but which to me seems appropriate) and capable of including a small Court Theatre in one of these wings and yet at the same time remaining utterly unassuming. The space is so vast that the proportions of the buildings remain gentle and harmonious and instead of the state coach, the wandering pedestrians and the red-coated troops which we find here in Canaletto's famous painting, I should not be surprised to see a yokel or an artisan, perhaps a saddler, perhaps a wheelwright, come out of an archway and cross the vast space which till then had been empty.

No close-up of the palace by itself can suggest the restfulness and dignity of this scene. Though its historical associations are so numerous, Maria Theresa, her son Joseph II, his sister Marie Antoinette, their niece Marie Louise, Napoleon, marriage connection cum foe who slept here in 1805 and 1809 and occupied the very room in which his son, the ill-fated King of Rome (renamed the Duc de Reichstadt by his Austrian grandfather) would die of consumption before he was twenty-one—these are only a few of the names, nevertheless the building is no mausoleum of lost hopes and lost dynasties; rather it still seems to invite occupation, and one would not be a bit surprised to see a great coach roll up to the door and Maria Theresa descend from it with a small instalment of her sixteen children.

I suggest that everybody should go in search of those children and find them in the incredibly fresh and beautiful pastels by Liotard which decorate several of the forty-four rooms in the central building which are shown to visitors. They can see the very embroideries which those children sewed to delight their mother on her birthday. And in the rooms once used as nurseries, full of light, and with Liotard's crayon evoking childhood in all its pink and fresh-complexioned and beribboned and post-Rousseau charm and spontaneity, it will seem that even time is unable to over-cloud this once happy past, and that the spirit of the nursery still lingers here, that Marie Antoinette is still a child with her hair drawn tightly back and tied with a blue bow, and that no poet has, as yet, stood in front of her dressing-table at Versailles and written his tragic quatrain:

> This was her table, these her trim outspread
> Brushes and trays and porcelain cups for red;
> Here sat she, while her women tired and curled
> The most unhappy head in all the world.

III

Vienna (continued)

You may safely banish all vain regrets for Fischer von Erlach's plans for Schönbrunn which were too grandiose to be put into execution, and may bless the memory of Paccassi, the Italian architect who completed the building as it now is, with a very special blessing for what he did with its interior. The style is the lively rococo of the eighteenth century, with an occasional emphasis on the exotic. But long before we come to the more exotic items, the Blue Drawing Room with its Chinese paper-hangings, or the Vieux-Laque Chamber with its lacquer-work panels with gold paintings, or the Napoleon Chamber with its huge Brussels tapestries with scenes from national life, or the quite astounding "Millionenzimmer", the Millions Room (because of its supposed cost in crowns), wainscoted with costly palisander wood and decorated with rococo ornaments enclosing priceless Persian and Indian miniatures, long before we have reached these, or the Grand Gallery (21), where those who came to the Congress of Vienna forgathered—"a place of human warmth and loveliness . . . a pastel of white and gold, with mirrors used discreetly, the walls brilliant with a thousand candle sconces"—we have been entranced, merely by what the rococo can do with variations on white and gold, in a succession of rooms that, for all the curves and filigrees, are essentially simple and restful (17). The earlier rooms—that is to say, earlier in the tour of the palace—are those occupied by the Emperor Franz Josef and his temperamental Empress. They have been left as occupied during their lifetime, and though we may admire the austerity of the Emperor's simple bedstead, on which he died in 1916, nearly everything in the furniture of these rooms reflects the indifferent taste of the mid-nineteenth century, just as everything in the castle of Arenenburg in Switzerland, whither ex-Queen Hortense retired with her son, the future Napoleon III, reflects it.

17　SCHÖNBRUNN PALACE:　The Chinese Room (*c.* 1750)

Fischer von Erlach, architect

18   SCHÖNBRUNN: The Main Façade, completed in 1750
Fischer von Erlach, architect

19   The Lower Belvedere (1716)
Lucas von Hildebrandt, architect

VIENNESE PALACES

Schönbrunn is not only an Aladdin's palace within; its vast grounds are an immense pleasance and a wonderful exemplar of baroque landscape gardening through which one can wander for hours and for days (10). The Gloriette stands where Fischer von Erlach had once planned that the palace itself should stand, looking down from the top of the hill across the Neptune fountains to the back of the palace along a wide, open green glade on either side of which avenues with immensely tall formal hedges, clipped in the French style, radiate out. The colonnade, which was only built in 1775 from plans by F. von Hohenberg, is strikingly dramatic against the background of sky which throws the winged statuary surmounting it into sharp relief. And in the grounds of Schönbrunn you will find the "Schoenen Brunner", the fountain from which the palace takes its name, the immensely high glass Palm House, and the Zoo, one of the oldest in Europe (1752), radiating out from its rather charming central pavilion in iron by Jadot much as the Menagerie of the Upper Belvedere radiates out in Kleiner's eighteenth-century engraving. Nearer afield is the Schönbrunner Schloss-Theater, where Marie Antoinette danced in the shepherd-and-shepherdess pastorals of the poet Metastasio and where Mozart conducted his opera *Der Schauspieldirektor*. The whole place is full of ghosts of the past, but they are happy ghosts like that of the elderly Franz Josef who reserved only one small rose garden at the side of the palace for his private use and who would set forth early each morning and walk through the grounds to the far side of the Zoo and then by way of a sloping green glade, dotted with apple trees and flowering shrubs, make his way to a small doorway in the park wall, to which he only had the key, on his way to visit Frau Schatt, the retired actress, whose friendship was—with the Empress's full approval—so precious to him.

Mr. Crankshaw is appreciative of Schönbrunn but on a note almost of patronage. Its beauty is "of a curious kind, thin perhaps, but cooling to the brain". It is "at least the extremely positive expression of a respectable point of view". Its exterior, "though not lacking in fineness, scarcely prepares one for the rioting extravagance concealed by that cool and non-committal front". This is grudging indeed when it comes to be compared with the eloquence of his description of the Belvedere: "The centre-piece of the fancy is the Upper Belvedere (12), standing on the hill top, and the gardens, falling away from the imposing doors, are arranged to display its charm as a jewel in an exquisite setting. . . . The northern aspect with the gardens descending from the topmost gravel terrace is, I suppose, the finest; but the south façade is no less beautiful. Entering the iron gates from a drab and rather noisy street, one is transported by the sudden vision of a fairy palace ornamented so profusely that the effect is one of an airy improvisation suddenly caught and held in stone. And there at one's feet is an artificial lake, a plain, unislanded expanse, reaching, it seems, to the very walls of the palace, which stands there lightly, like an image in a dream, aloof beyond the mirror-shallow pool." It is all true, but those three words "ornamented so profusely" are in my eyes the Belvedere's condemnation by comparison with Schönbrunn. I prefer the small, simple, utterly graceful and gracious Lower Belvedere (19), which is almost as modest in appearance as Maria Theresa's stables in another part of the city (now used for Vienna's annual fair), to the Upper Belvedere, that great building at the top of the hill built between 1700 and 1723 for Prince Eugene, the victor of the Turkish Wars, by Lucas von Hildebrandt (16). The site is beautiful, the immense terraced park with its fountains and statuary is beautiful, the wonderful wrought-iron gates are beautiful, the building itself, with its great breadth and its four wing towers with their ornamental roofs, is beautiful. But it is just a shade too beautiful. That is to say, ostentation has crept in. Baroque, which can afford to be exuberant, since that is basic to its nature, can never afford to be ostentatious, for then what has only barely managed to be a virtue becomes instantly a vice. And if the exterior of the Upper Belvedere is not ostentatious, and I am afraid that it is, then the interior certainly is (13). Instead of winning you by sheer beauty as the Schönbrunn interiors do, it shouts at you, and the words which it shouts are: "Have you ever seen anything so magnificent as this? Could a staircase go further and remain a staircase at all? Open your eyes and gape, because that is what you are here to do." No wonder that as soon as Prince Eugene of Savoy, who was himself a member of an ancient reigning family and had saved Vienna from destruction, had died, the Hapsburgs had to buy it and add it to their other possessions. It was here that the Archduke Franz Ferdinand was residing with his morganatic wife Sophie Choteck just before they set forth to Sarajevo to meet their death, thereby plunging Europe into an era of hatred, bloodshed and destruction such as it had not known for nearly a century. If after their first escape in the streets of that frontier town—for a bomb had been thrown and had left them scatheless—the chauffeur had not over-shot the turning and instead of going on stopped the car to retrace the way, would no student have jumped on the running board and blazed away with his revolver at husband and wife, would there be Hapsburgs still living at Schönbrunn and the Belvedere, and would Europe have turned back from the madness which was to overtake it to that relative sanity which it still enjoyed in 1913?

Not one person in twenty thousand, I imagine, thinks of Franz Ferdinand to-day when they visit the Upper Belvedere, which is the apotheosis of eighteenth-century glory and not of twentieth-century disaster. The Marmorsaal with its decorations of stucco and Salzburg marble and its ceiling paintings by Altomonte and Gaetano Fanti, the great staircase, the rooms embellished by the handiwork of a Bussi or a Drentwett, it is all very fine, but when you have said that you have said everything—it is all very fine but . . .? I prefer the Lower Belvedere where Eugene had the sense to die, in preference to the great building at the top of the hill. Mr. Crankshaw describes it as "utilitarian, a low, cool, rambling affair of stucco", but in actual fact its lines are simple and gracious, it cannot be said to ramble a great deal, and it is nearly as austere and straightforward as the neighbouring Orangerie, which too has my approval. The Marmorsaal of the Lower Belvedere is ornate, but most of the other rooms are simple enough and make a fine setting for the treasures of the Baroque Museum which now decorate them (23, 24).

One can amuse oneself turning partisan and weighing the merits of Schönbrunn against those of the Upper Belvedere, though different tastes might give a completely different verdict. But one cannot weigh the merits of Vienna's greatest palace of all, the Hofburg, in any scale or by any known standard, because it is not a building at all but an assemblage of buildings, of the most heterogeneous nature, spread over six centuries. It must cover a very respectable acreage and its *Trakte* or wings extend in a number of directions and generally enclose courtyards. The oldest part of the building dates from the Babenberg days of the thirteenth century, but the façade, which is most imposing (though not necessarily most pleasing) and which must be soon familiar to anyone who sets foot in Vienna, is that which was planned by Semper and Hasenauer and begun in 1881 and which despite its vast and towering proportions is only part of an unfinished scheme which was to have enclosed the Heldenplatz. From the colonnaded façade an ex-house-painter screamed the announcement of his triumphant occupation of Austria, thereby ensuring—though his clairvoyance did not extend so far—that Lenin and Stalin's portraits should hang, incongruously posed against an equally incongruous red cloth star, on the face of the building a few years later, with an effect not dissimilar to that of a poster on the flanks of Westminster Abbey. It is regrettable that those who feel it to be their mission in life to sow the wind cannot be given an occasional preview of the subsequent whirlwind.

As their town residence down the centuries the Hofburg has enough Hapsburg family history attached to it to fill volumes. The ruling family could watch Vienna from its windows and Vienna could more or less watch them—in fact, the colonels of one regiment which had acted with commendable promptitude on a certain occasion had ever afterwards the privilege of entering the Emperor's own room unannounced. The Michaelertrakt, to the designs of Fischer von Erlach the Younger, the Schweizerhof, so named because it was guarded by Maria Theresa's Swiss troops, the Schweizertor, a Renaissance gateway (1552) with coloured coats-of-arms, inscriptions and painted frescoes under its archway, the Burgkapelle, the Amalientrakt, begun under Maximilian II in 1575 and whose last occupant was the beautiful Empress Elizabeth, and the Reichskanzleitrakt, where were the former private apartments of her spouse, the Emperor Franz Josef, all deserve attention. But the two highlights of this immense cluster of buildings, for the more hurried

visitor at least, are the library, and the Leopoldinischetrakt with
its ceremonial rooms, which owe their charm, as at Schönbrunn,
to the rococo and to Maria Theresa, whose bedroom was one of
them and whose bed you can see under a great hook in the ceiling
with a pulley across which a rope was passed so that she could
hoist herself up in bed. The rooms, including the Pietradura
Room with Franz I's wonderful collection of Florentine stone
pictures, are now the President's, when he sleeps in Vienna,
and they are full of surpassingly beautiful historical treasures,
miniatures and pastels by Liotard (there is a magnificent one,
which I will go bail is wholly his, of Maria Christine, mother of
the great Empress, a courageous-looking old lady with pink
cheeks, white hair and a black handkerchief over her head), as
well as a clock from Darmstadt given by the Landgrave of Hesse
to Maria Theresa for her silver wedding in 1761, with a complete
drama of heaven and earth, demons and guardian angels and
happy pair, enacted in pantomime on its immense silver front
when the hour strikes, a toy smaller but quite as elaborate in its
own way as its later descendant, the famous Guinness clock in
the Festival Gardens. We are abashed by the beauty, grace and
novelty of it all, just as we were abashed at Schönbrunn, for
everything the great Empress possessed seems to be lovely and
personal and unique and to be still protected by the aura of
connoisseurship in which it was first born.

The other high-light is the world-famous National Library
(20), which occupies one side of the Josefsplatz, looking down
on Zauner's bronze equestrian statue of the Emperor Josef II. I
cannot wholly agree with Sacheverell Sitwell when he says in
German Baroque Art that the Hofbibliothek is "the finest achievement of Fischer's life" or that "this is the finest library design
in the world". He may be right, but as a great booklover (and I
can claim to be one) I think I would prefer to find myself reading
daily in the library at Admont or at Einsiedeln, each of them a
triumph of the baroque, but lighter, less huge, less over-
whelming. The Hofbibliothek, commissioned in 1722 by the
Emperor Karl VI, is nobly conceived; both the Fischers had a
hand in it, as well as Pacassi. The domed, oval central hall, with
its pair of white pillars either end, is a masterpiece of baroque

63

interior decoration, and Daniel Gran's frescoes are harmonious as they look down on *inter alia* the great gilt-titled leather tomes from the library of Prince Eugene of Savoy. Here, as in so much that we meet in Vienna, the eighteenth century is made to seem the climax of our civilisation and all that has supervened, including ourselves, a rather uncertain anticlimax. For the basis of civilisation is confidence in the future, and its attendant arts are only really happy when convinced that there will always be someone to enjoy them, always someone to protect them from destruction by vandals.

The Vienna which Canaletto painted in 1759 was spacious, gracious and leisurely, the periphery of the city as important as its centre; all the delights of rural life within easy walking distance for any citizen who felt disposed to enjoy them.

My compatriot, the Irishman Michael Kelly, who for four years from 1783 was engaged to sing at the Court Theatre in Vienna and who was the friend of Mozart and appeared in the first production of *Figaro,* has much to tell us of the capital towards the end of the great Empress's reign. The Vienna of that time was a place "where pleasure was the order of the day and night. The women, generally speaking, are beautiful; they have fine complexions, and symmetrical figures, the lower orders particularly. All the servant-maids are anxious to show their feet (which are universally handsome) and are very ambitious of having neat shoes and stockings."

Of the ridotto rooms where the masquerades took place he writes: "I never saw, or indeed heard, of any suite of rooms where elegance and convenience were more considered: for the propensity of the Vienna ladies for dancing and going to carnival masquerades was so determined, that nothing was permitted to interfere with their enjoyment of their favourite amusement—nay, so notorious was it, that for the sake of ladies in the family way, who could not be persuaded to stay at home, there were apartments with every convenience for their accouchement, should they unfortunately be required. And I have been gravely told, and almost believe, that there have actually been instances of the utility of the arrangement." Kelly's various encounters with the Emperor Joseph II are well described (thanks, it is said, to Theodore Hook who ghosted his book) and convincing. He writes: "One evening, at one of these masquerades, a well-turned compliment was paid to the Emperor, by a gentleman who went in the character of Diogenes with his lantern in search of a man. In going round the room, he suddenly met the Emperor. He immediately made a low obeisance to His Majesty, and, opening his lantern, extinguishing the candle, saying in a loud tone, 'Ho trovato l'uomo' (I have found the man); he then took his departure and left the ballroom. He was said to have been a courtier, but none of the courtiers would admit he was." If he was not, he deserved to be.

The Vienna which Kelly knew was shortly to expand. The great families who in the eighteenth century built their summer palaces not in distant provinces but just outside the capital set an example to the bourgeois who followed upon the Napoleonic wars and who with a comfortable balance at the bank began to build themselves relatively modest but very pleasant villas in the outskirts. The Biedermeier period—which one might translate as the Smith-Jones period—early in the nineteenth century, is, like so much else, enshrined in the hearts of the Viennese, who have a sentimental affection for it, intelligible but not wholly justified by all its products. Karl Werner has written: "The Biedermeier was a period of a personal culture of living, it was a time of man and not of the state", and this happy flowering of individuality is symbolised in Moritz von Schwind's lithographs of "The Picnic on the Leopoldsberg", or Kupelwieser's water-colour of the Schubertians playing at Atzenbrugg, where young Vienna is represented as relaxing in a world freed at last from the horror of wars and invasions, and with the dark shadow of Napoleon, dictator even to Hapsburg pride, at last removed. "When the day's work was done—and no one was spared from it, for even the writers were all honourable civil servants—the Viennese character showed itself in the delight in enjoyment. The whole year was filled with small and large-scale entertainments, music and dancing. Most Viennese felt an urge—which needed no excuse—to visit coffee houses and restaurants, theatres and concerts almost daily. Their style of living was adapted accordingly. A public discussion among a circle of

friends of a newly published book was preferred to a quiet
reading of it.'' * An idyllic epoch, which nevertheless would
have let Schubert starve to death but for the help of one or two
devoted adherents who were not in a position themselves to do
very much for him. For behind the villa, behind the picnics in
the country, behind the carefree young people was Papa and his
bank balance and his far from impeccable taste in furniture. I
cannot agree with Werner when he asks: ''But what is the
Biedermeier style if not the style of tasteful simplification?'' In
Dr. Sobek's delightful Biedermeier home in Vienna which he
has furnished with a collection of treasures and association items
of the period, I have seen many pieces that were intrinsically
lovely (generally, it should be added, under earlier Empire
influence) but others, such as bulging mahogany flower-stands, or
huge, heavy receptacles for newspapers, made of the same wood,
which were grotesquely ugly and which bear witness to a taste at
once childish and atrocious. It is obvious that the people who
bought these things and for whom they were created were in-
capable of passing an æsthetic judgment and bought them either
because of a childish pride in their novelty or for their ostentatious contribution to the so-called comfort of life. The best of
Biedermeier is light and gracious and lyrical, and some of the
ceilings and interior decoration and porcelain or tiled stoves are
charming, variations really on what are still eighteenth-century
themes; but most of its innovations are ominous and if one wished
to be really unkind one would label this the era of cast iron and
mahogany.

Biedermeier brings us to the threshold of mid-nineteenth-
century Vienna, to the creation of the Ringstrasse, and to the
last great burst of architectural activity, apart from the vast
municipal undertakings on behalf of the workers, which were
undertaken by the Social Democrats after the first world war.
On December 30, 1857, Franz Josef put his signature to the
document ordering the bastions to be raised and the *glacis*
levelled. It is significant, as John Lehmann points out, that the
buildings which now came into existence were not churches or
palaces (if we except the unfinished extension for the Hofburg,

* Richard Smekal.

28   VIENNA: The National Library (Hofbibliothek) (1723–35)
Fischer von Erlach, architect

21 SCHÖNBRUNN PALACE: The "Grosse Galerie" (c. 1750)

Fischer von Erlach, architect

and the Votive Church, a neo-Gothic structure of which modern Viennese are almost unduly scornful, which was begun in 1856 at the instigation of the unfortunate Archduke Maximilian, Franz Josef's brother, to commemorate the Emperor's escape from assassination). Instead, as Lehmann tells us, "the Ring offers a pretty panorama of the ideals of the nineteenth-century liberal bourgeoisie, with its new University, State Opera House, Burgtheater, Rathaus, Stock Exchange, Parliament, Palace of Justice and Museums. Many architects took part in this work, and in an age without a style their numbers only made the æsthetic confusion worse. Siccardsburg and Van der Nüll's vast Opera House, with its Italian Renaissance motifs, stands at the traffic centre of the new Vienna, at the crossing of the Kärtnerstrasse and the Ring, where it can impose itself without rivals. But a little further along by the Burg-Tor style begins to jostle style roughly and startlingly. Theophil von Hausen's Hellenic Parliament House next to Ferstel's vaguely Renaissance Burgtheater, and towering above both of them Schmidt's Gothic Rathaus, reminiscent of the cloth-halls of Belgium. At the same time, in between these giants, rows of new dwelling-houses and shops were erected that seem characterless enough and are yet, taken together, characteristic of their age, as the occasional introduction of a later building shows."

It is difficult to modify or qualify this, beyond saying that when we look at these buildings their historical context is perhaps still too much uppermost in our minds and that if we could judge them intrinsically, forgetting history, and forgetting also their unfortunate juxtaposition, they would almost certainly have more merit in our eyes. The white marble Parliament building with its ramp in front, its four bronze groups of horse tamers, its seated Greek and Roman historians and its line of statues against the sky (striking at any time but most so against the milky white of a late afternoon sky before sunset) has much to be said in its favour, and the huge Pallas Athene Fountain immediately in front is appropriate and finely conceived. Other cities present equally curious architectural juxtapositions, even if they are spread over a longer period of time. One authority declares that all these buildings reflect something of the mid-nineteenth-century enthusiasm of those who created them, "who built thus in honour of a dawn which turned out to be a sunset". This grim phrase is only another way of saying that we look at them now with the cold eye of later disillusion, and are resentful that, despite their various intermediate vicissitudes, they appear as solid and assured as ever, reminders of man creative in contrast to man destructive.

In the Rathaus is the Historical Museum of Vienna to kindle the enthusiasm of those who value the city's long and dramatic past. And if we cross the Rathaus Platz, where Sonnenfels figures a little incongruously among the eight statues of men famous in the history of Vienna, and enter the Volksgarten (where we will find the thoughtful Grillparzer sitting in an alcove with draperies over his knees under an imposing Greek portico flanked by reliefs from his different plays), we can make our way past the open-air Restaurant Tirolgarten, once favoured by the Crown Prince Rudolf, and emerge on the Ring, not far from the Maria Theresien Platz where the great Empress sits high above the equestrian statues of her four most famous army commanders. It is a fine piece of work, more elaborate than but almost as fine in its way as the two magnificent equestrian bronzes of Prince Eugene and the Archduke Karl (victor over Napoleon in 1809) in the Heldenplatz, both by Anton Fernkorn, who, imaginative Viennese will tell you, but quite untruly, committed suicide because having made the Archduke's reined-in mount rear successfully on its two hind legs without further support, he found himself obliged in the case of Prince Eugène to achieve stability with the aid of the charger's magnificently heavy tail. A horse balanced on its tail is apparently nearly as grave an offence in a sculptor as a Cockney rhyme is for a poet.

Flanking either side of the Maria Theresien Platz are the Natural History Museum and the History of Art Museum, imposing edifices built in the 1870's to designs by Semper, in the style of the Italian high-Renaissance. The Art Museum houses a magnificent collection beginning with Egypt and covering the centuries, and even those who, by choice or from necessity, take their museums at a hand gallop should not miss the Sieger statue, a fifth-century Greek bronze found at Magdalenenberge in

Carinthia in 1502, which Dürer journeyed to see, and which with its grace and lightness and the serene gesture of its upraised right hand must have amply rewarded him for his journey, being assuredly one of the most beautiful Greek male statues in existence; or Dürer's own portrait of a young Venetian painted three years later in 1505, a ringletted girl in a low-cut dress with bi-coloured ribbon shoulder-knots, whose amused, reflective brown eyes and full-lipped and very slightly ironic half-smile put the simpering mask of the "Mona Lisa" to immediate shame; or the many superb Breughels, or Bronzino's "Holy Family", lovelier even than the magnificent Bronzino in the London National Gallery; or Tintoretto's "Susanna and the Elders", a canvas that makes praise even by superlatives seem beggarly in relation to its stupendous merits. It would be worth crossing Europe to see these alone, just as it would be worth crossing the Atlantic to spend two or three days at the Albertina studying the drawings in the collection made by the Archduke Albert of Sachsen-Teschen (whose name may mean little to us but who must stand honoured for his discrimination so long as his collection shall remain in being), works of incomparable worth by Dürer and Rubens as well as by Rembrandt, Fragonard and others.

The visitor to Vienna must make his own choice amidst such riches, a choice based partly on the time at his disposal and partly on his personal predilections. Happy the man or woman who is not pressed for time and who can come to this city and pursue unhurried his or her particular cultural interest. Perhaps he is interested in the baroque and will hasten forth to the Neuer Markt to see the Donnerbrunnen, the fountain which is considered by many to be Raphael Donner's finest work and the best conception for a fountain in all Vienna. It was finished in 1739 and when restored in 1873 the lead figures were replaced by bronze copies. In the centre four *putti* play around a pedestal on which stands Providence, and along the rim of the wide basin rest the figures of the four rivers Enns, March, Traun and Ybbs. They are superbly modelled, patterned in some degree on antiquity, but really illustrating the specific virtues of the baroque at its best, in what might be termed a mood of strictly-restrained exuberance. In fact the river Enns—the original is to

be found in the Baroque Museum in the Lower Belvedere—
might be made a test piece. If you do not like it you are never
likely to be converted to baroque sculpture. Pevsner says that by
the time Donner made his fountain the storm of baroque had
blown over and calm had set in and that he was really a pioneer
in a new movement towards neo-classicism; but this is perhaps
just another way of saying that here baroque is on its guard
against its own excesses and has refused to be carried away by
them.

I have made no mention as yet of Vienna in relation to music,
for nothing is more distressing to a writer than to know that he
has at his disposal about half a page to devote to a topic that really
demands an entire book. Vienna has been the Mecca of musicians
and the home for generation after generation of genuine and most
ardent music lovers. You can still hear opera sung in Vienna in a
way that I believe you can hear it nowhere else in the whole
world, for the singing seems to be genuinely effortless: these
artists do not appear to have to worry about their voices at all,
they are *dramatis personæ* whose thoughts and emotions simply
overflow into song as the most natural and convenient mode of
self-expression. And so the charm of *Figaro,* the humour of
Figaro, the melody of *Figaro* all blend into a unity, and this not
by any apparent striving but as though it were second nature on
the part of the singers. No wonder that, though the Stefansdom
took precedence of it, the Viennese soon set to work to rebuild
both their famous Opera House and their Burgtheater when
these suffered disaster in the second world war. Meanwhile
the charming little Theater an der Wien, where Schikaneder
delighted the Viennese of his day with Mozart's *Magic Flute* by
writing the text and directing the first production, and where
Beethoven's *Fidelio* had its first performance in 1805, became,
together with the Volksoper, the temporary home of State
Opera. I found once in the Nationalbibliothek a delightful little
coloured engraving of a rural landscape with a bare-kneed
musician in blue stockings, hat in hand and carrying his instrument under his arm, leaving the sunny portico of what appeared
to be an inn beside some Alpine stream. This Arcadian scene
really represented Anton Hasenhut leaving the Theater an der

Wien, the very theatre in which I had been listening to music
only the night before; but since the river Wien is now covered
for much of its course through the city my error was perhaps
excusable.

Stefan Zweig has said that art always reaches its peak when it
becomes the life interest of a people. Maria Theresa employed
Gluck to teach her daughters music. Joseph II would discuss
Mozart's operas with him ("You must admit, my dear Mozart,
there are a great many notes." "But not too many, Sire."—a
reply which admirers of *Figaro* will be ready to endorse).
Leopold III himself composed music, but the later Emperors took
no interest in it, and Franz Josef is said to have had almost an
antipathy for it, hinting to Mahler on one occasion that it was
quite unreasonable to expect people who had come to the opera
to talk, to forgo this justifiable activity. But what the court
abandoned, the population of Vienna took into its guardianship,
becoming one of the most enthusiastic and at the same time
most critical audiences in the world—"every flat note was
remarked, every incorrect intonation and every cut were
censured; and this control was exercised at premières not by the
professional critics alone, but day after day by the entire audience,
whose attentive ears had been sharpened by constant
comparison".

Vienna has produced few writers, none, it has been pointed
out, in the first rank. Grillparzer, the friend of Schubert, whose
dark-blue eyes cast such a spell on the daughter of the Prussian
ambassador that she admitted the fact in her will and bequeathed
her picture to him, and who, distrusting his capacity for marriage,
waited until he was eighty-two to become betrothed to Katherina
Froehlich, although he had made the home of the sisters his
own for thirty years previous to this, is a poetic dramatist too
much in bondage to national themes to have become a European
figure.

But if the writers are few the musicians are many and highly
honoured. Grillparzer as a child had sat on the knee of a servant
girl whose proudest boast was that she had had a walking-on part
in Mozart's *Magic Flute*. One could make Vienna the scene of an
exclusively musical pilgrimage if one so wished. One can

encounter Gluck at Schönbrunn and Haydn in the Mariahilf district, the house in which he died, No. 19 Haydngasse, being now a Haydn museum. Though Gluck owed most to Italian and French influences, it was Vienna which appointed him presently Composer for Theatre and Chamber Music, and Vienna for whom he would write *Orpheus* (1762), *Alceste* (1767), and *Paris and Helen* (1770). Haydn came to Vienna at the age of eight as a *Sängerknabe*, but when his voice began to break his choirmaster was quick to turn him into the street, where a church vocalist named Spangler found him half-starving and probably saved the life of the man who years later, on a visit to England, would be offered a poem, *The Creation*, to set to music, and who would kneel daily and pray to God to sustain the burst of inspiration which had then overtaken him, until he had finished the task of writing the score. Hans Gal has said: "There is no profounder expression of the philosophical ideals of eighteenth-century rationalism than the perfect, logical order of a string quartet or symphony of Haydn. Our world, created by God on a pre-stabilised harmony, is the best of all possible worlds. This, the quintessence of Leibnitz's philosophy, is not only the clearly stated main idea of Haydn's greatest work, *The Creation*. It stands, an unwritten motto, on every page of his music, a creed based on the sublime confidence that, if only Reason would prevail, universal happiness would be round the nearest corner." "If only"—those two crucial words carry upon them the whole weight of mankind's misery, and must do so, one is sometimes tempted to think, until the end of time.

Mozart dedicated his finest set of string quartets to Haydn, and the latter could say to Leopold Mozart, the father, "I declare before God, as a man of honour, that your son is the greatest composer of whom I have ever heard." Haydn had influenced the younger man and was in turn influenced by him before his death. Mozart settled in Vienna as a free-lance in 1781. Beethoven paid his first visit to the city as a young man in 1787, the year in which Mozart was appointed as *Kammer-Compositeur* to the Imperial Court, receiving a small yearly salary in return for composing dance music for the Imperial *Redouten* Balls. Haydn would accept Beethoven as a pupil, referring to him as The

Grand Mogul. So we see how, though they were never intimates, the lives of these great men were interlaced.

One can seek the shade of Beethoven not only in the Vienna woods where he loved to walk, or in the Beethoven House on the Pfarrplatz in Heiligenstadt—where you can go and drink Heuriger, the new wine of the season, under the roof beneath which was composed the Pastoral Symphony—or in the Schwarz-spanierstrasse where is the house in which the composer died, but in at least a dozen other haunts as well; just as you can seek out Schubert at 54 Nussdorferstrasse, which was once his birth-place and is now a museum, or Brahms on the Karlsgasse, or Bruckner on the Schottenring, or Lanner, or the two Johann Strausses, or Hugo Wolf, or Mahler, or (briefer visitants) Liszt and Schumann and Wagner and Sibelius, on all of whom at some time or other Vienna cast a measure of its enchantment. Indeed it would take some days to make the rounds of the musical monuments and commemorative statues in the city, from Haydn, type of eighteenth-century dignity and propriety, in the busy Mariahilferstrasse, to Strauss who is to be found playing his violin under a rather exotic white marble arch of figures in vague relief in the gardens of the left bank of the river Wien.

Indeed we will enjoy Vienna most when we shed all sense of obligation and allow our ramblings to become capricious and even chaotic. What shall we do this morning? We can wander into the Heldenplatz and sniff the scent of lilac which drifts to-wards us on the air from neighbouring public gardens, and be presently carried where our mood directs us. Why not go and see the famous tablecloth on which Anna Sacher, the proprietress of the Hotel Sacher, got almost every European celebrity of her day to write his or her name? Or let the tablecloth wait, for we have not yet seen the Church of St. Maria-am-Gestade, which stands near where the Danube once flowed (hence its popularity in those days as a place of worship for salt-shippers), and which is more important and beautiful than a wilderness of tablecloths. Its lovely west portal, its seven-sided tower, rich late-Gothic, the open tracery of its fine stone cupola, and its gargoyles are all worth seeing, as well as the Gothic statues which decorate its columns within. No? We are church-saturated? Now is the moment perhaps to have a look at L'Ecurie Impériale and to admire its straightforward, gracious lines, so evocative of that eighteenth century for which Fischer von Erlach created them, or to make our way to the back of the Hofburg to the Winter-reitschule, the stables of the Spanish Riding School, with its great riding hall decorated in white and with forty-six Corinthian columns to support its gallery. Here the white Lippiza stallions displayed their accomplishments: the pirouette, levade, crouvade, ballotade and capriole, to finish with the jump into the air "on the spot", that last word in equine adaptability. The Hapsburgs loved their horses. Franz Josef stuck to them to the end, and was not to be seduced from this loyalty by Edward VII, who visited him in 1909 and showed him his newly acquired open motor car of which he was so proud. Only in 1915, as a gesture in face of current Viennese distress in wartime, would Florian, the favourite white stallion, have to demean himself by drawing a milk car.

The name of the Riding School recalls the Hapsburg link with Spain. So, although many are unaware of it, does the Prater, for the Viennese seized on the Spanish word *prado* meaning meadow and converted it to describe what was originally a jealously guarded game preserve for the high nobility. The latter were not at all pleased when Joseph II threw a large part open to the public who would one day enter into happy and almost complete possession, their proprietary rights symbolised by the Riesenrad (Giant Wheel), which might have come straight from Coney Island, and perhaps did. It stands in the Volks- or Wurstelprater amid swings, merry-go-rounds, grottoes and switchback railways, a Brobdingnagian variation of that spirit which created Wurstel (Punch) to amuse children; and when the second world war was drawing to its close and this ground was being fiercely fought over, this colossal wheel, with its series of little hanging carriages, standing up stark and unpainted against the sky, must have seemed to the soldiers of at least half a dozen nations the pathetic sign-token of a frivolity that had vanished and might never again return. To-day the Prater is green and gracious again, and on a Sunday afternoon its famous chestnut avenue, its restaurants and tea-gardens echo once more to the laughter of children.

22 VIENNA: The Karlskirche (1717)

Fischer von Erlach, architect

23 "The River Enns", deta
from the Neuer Markt Fountai
(1737–39)
Raphael Donner, sculptor

24 A marble figure in th
Marmorgalerie

When Joseph II opened the Prater to the public his nobles complained that they would no longer find themselves among their equals. The Emperor replied cuttingly, "If I always wished to be among my equals I should be forced to take my walks in the Kapuzinergruft, among the deceased Hapsburgs." Though a pilgrimage to the Kaisergruft (Imperial Crypt) beneath the Church of the Capuchins is almost as complete an antithesis as could be conceived to a morning spent pacing the sunny leaf-traceried sidewalks of the Prater, any tourist who leaves Vienna without making it has made a grave mistake. It is almost a *pièce de résistance* with professional guides, who after expounding to the open-mouthed of several nations that only the corpse of a particular member of the Imperial Family rests here, the heart being deposited at the Augustinian Church and the viscera at St. Stefan's, will then add slyly, "I know what you are smiling at. You are thinking that at the last day they will have trouble to bring their things together!"

The crypt and its contents would impress even an ancient Egyptian, although he might scorn these magnificently ornate and elaborate coffins on the ground that they are not of gold but only of lead and pewter and, in the later instances, of bronze: 141 persons are interred in 138 sarcophagi in the crypt, among them twelve emperors and fifteen empresses, so that a visit to the original crypt and its various later extensions—the last the Franz Josef Tomb and the New Crypt Chapel built by the architect Cajo Perisic in 1908-9—is like taking a trip through history for more than three hundred years. I do not suggest that the crypt is the ideal introduction to the baroque, although B. F. Moll's amazing tomb for the Empress Maria Theresa and her consort is a masterpiece of its kind, and figures like that of "Mourning Austria" on his tomb for her father Karl VI, or his reflective cherub supporting a medallion of one of the archduchesses, are quite superb and would grace any museum of art. Franz Ferdinand could not come here because of his morganatic wife and is buried beside her at Artstettin; but one person of less than imperial lineage lies amongst this august assemblage. She is the Countess Fuchs, Maria Theresa's governess. You can see her portrait hanging upon the wall at Schönbrunn, and it was the Empress's

wish—one more illustration of that essentially domestic sentiment which probably helped to sustain this much-wronged
woman—that all the rules of the game were broken so that she
might lie here not far from her imperial mistress.

It is the historical associations which make a visit to the crypt
so interesting. Figure after famed figure rests here. You will not
find Marie Antoinette. No one knows where she lies. Nor will
you find Napoleon's son, variously named the King of Rome, the
Duc de Reichstadt, L'Aiglon, whose coffin after being here for
over one hundred years was despatched to Paris in 1940 to rest
beside that of his father, a gesture duly discounted, one imagines,
in view of its circumstances, by the French. But you will find,
side by side, in tragic proximity, the coffins of a wife, a husband
and a son—Elizabeth, Franz Josef, Rudolf—and if you remember
anything of their history you may kneel, as I have done, at the
prie-dieu nearby, to whisper your prayer for those two restless,
ill-fated souls, that of the mother who would die by an assassin's
hand, and that of the son who would die by his own; and for that
other long-suffering and astonishingly staunch one who would
outlive them both.

> Lie down, lie down, young yeoman,
> The sun moves always west.
> The road thou treadst to labour
> Will lead thee home to rest,
> And that will be the best.

It is not only to yeomen that it may seem the best. It may have
seemed so even to that dauntless eighty-six-year-old who despite
three days of bronchitis and temperature, which he had fought
on his feet, went to bed at last on the afternoon of Wednesday,
November 22nd, 1916, saying to his valet Ketterl, "Please call
me at half-past three to-morrow. I am behindhand with my
work." About nine o'clock that night he wakened with a fit of
coughing. The valet raised him in bed, punched his pillows and
brewed a quick cup of tea, which he cooled by pouring it into
and back from the cup. The old Emperor watched him with
dimming eyes. "Ich danke Dir, Ketterl," he gasped as he gulped
it down. These were his last words. On November 30th, 1916,

the funeral cortège—funeral not only of an emperor but of an empire—moved along the Ringstrasse on its way to the Crypt of the Capuchins. The Master of Ceremonies, whose duty at Schönbrunn had always been to announce the coming of the Emperor to his waiting guests, lifts his baton and knocks three times on the locked door of the monastery. A voice from within enquires, "Who demands entry?" "His Apostolic Majesty, the Kaiser Franz." And the monk replies, "I do not know him." The mace is lifted again. "The sovereign Kaiser Franz wishes to be admitted." "I do not know him," the monk repeats, and adds, "In the Name of God, who wishes to enter?" The Master of Ceremonies replies, "Your brother Franz, a poor sinner", and the door of the crypt swings slowly back to allow the coffin of Franz Josef to join those of his ancestors.

IV

Lower Austria

I HAVE not, in the previous two chapters, wasted my reader's time dwelling on the gastronomic delights of Vienna, on its fashions and frivolities, and on the whole "Wiener Lebensart" —the Viennese manner of living—pleasurable discoveries, but best made by each individual for himself, according to circumstance, and scarcely needing any dithyramb from me to introduce them. Had I space I might have enlarged on the warm and homely comfort of the Stamm Café as an institution, on fried chicken and Wiener Schnitzel, on that apotheosis of the doughnut the Faschingskrapfen, or on the Sachertorte, which we owe to Metternich's solicitude for his guests at a very special banquet. It was not of Sachertorte assuredly that the great chancellor was thinking when a very handsome Austrian baron courageously hid him in his carriage and drove him at walking pace through the infuriated mob who, ignorant of his presence amongst them, were howling for his blood, when revolution broke out in Vienna in 1848. The baron's name was Charles von Hügel, a great soldier and an even greater botanist, and in his fifty-fifth year he would marry a Scotch girl, Elizabeth Farquharson, in her twentieth and by her become the father of that much loved scholar and "saint" Frederick von Hügel, the loyal son of a church who should one day make him the patron saint of speculative minds, if such persons can be allowed a patron saint.

Equally neglected with Viennese food have been the Viennese suburbs, for the temptation to thrust them out of their already overcrowded context, as part of the city, into my chapter upon the province of Lower Austria, was irresistible. As it is I leave the Capital inevitably with a sense of guilt, deeply conscious of many sins of omission, buildings at which we should have peered, people of whom we should have tried to get a glimpse, as for example the Viennese-born ballerina Fanny Elssler. She wins my heart in old engravings and in Cyril Beaumont's monograph,

and I am delighted by that simplicity of manners which made
her and her sister drink only water at a great banquet given
for them by a French impresario and select a modest hatpin and
a little handbag from the great tray of jewelled presents which
were carried round to the guests. Perhaps as we go out of the city
we may meet her in the Vienna woods in a setting appropriate to
her grace and modesty; just as I should like to meet the astounding
child, Fritz Kreisler, with the devoted doctor father who was an
amateur musician himself but who abandoned each instrument
that he played a little sadly, when his infant prodigy of a child
overtook him, until at last he was left only with the viola.

Vienna would normally be the capital of the province of
Lower Austria if it were not to-day a "province" itself, the only
one of the nine which has not at some point a frontier with a
foreign nation, being enclosed in Niederösterreich like the pearl
in an oyster. The city has kept its bonds of intimacy with the
surrounding country in a way that cities like London and New
York long ago ceased to do. The Wienerwald so well loved by
Beethoven, and where Strauss got his inspiration for his *Tales
from the Vienna Woods*, can be reached easily, even by those who
have no car, in as little as thirty minutes by tramcar. The vines
grow on the lower slopes of these famed hills, and the white
wine from them is drunk by the Viennese in the local "Heuriger"
taverns when the season arrives. Each tavern, when it has pressed
its own new wine, hangs out on a pole a wreath of evergreens or
a branch of fir as a sign-token that the wine is now being drunk
on the premises, and out come families and groups of friends
from the city, bringing in many cases their own cold sausage and
picnic fare, to sit there drinking the new thin white wine,
singing or listening to the music of the tavern's "Schrammel"
quartet, consisting of a first and second violin, a guitar and an
accordion player. In the silent streets, flanked by their small
eighteenth-century and nineteenth-century one-storey houses,
at Grinzing, there is nothing to suggest festivity, on some night
late in September, least of all the groups of cars upon which one
comes from time to time and which have a mysterious and completely abandoned look. But enter a courtyard, push open a door
and catch the first strains of some Viennese "Heuriger" song,

and at those thronged tables strewn with food packages and surrounded by flushed, happy faces you will find what you were looking for, a tradition of homely enjoyment that goes right back to the time of Schubert and far beyond.

One can drive out from Vienna along the Wiener Hoehenstrasse, which was begun in 1934 and finished two years later, to visit the two great viewpoints over the city and its environs, the Kahlenberg and the Leopoldsberg; or one can join this fine road from Grinzing and get a foretaste of the scenery on the terrace at Kobenzl, in front of what was once an eighteenth-century palace built for the statesman Count Kobenzl and is now an hotel with an adjoining, very modern, but finely-designed, circular bar and café which fulfils not only these functions but that of viewpoint at the same time.

From Kobenzl the road winds slowly upwards between the trees, until at a little over 1,400 feet the Kahlenberg is reached, the point from which the Turkish siege of Vienna was raised in 1683 by Polish and Imperial troops. Vienna had been under fire for sixty days and nights; the Turks with the aid of French fortification engineers were tunnelling under the walls and earthworks, and demolishing the defences sector by sector; food was running short and the forces of the defenders were so depleted that they found it hard to keep the city streets clear of the bodies of the dead, when on the night of September 10th a horseman managed to swim the Danube with Starhemberg's last appeal for aid to Charles of Lorraine: "Lose no further time, Lord, on no account lose more time." The Duke lost no time. His forces, 27,000 Austrians, 20,000 Poles and nearly 33,000 Saxons, Bavarians, Swabians and Franks, were already crossing the Danube at Tulln and Krems and next night he camped on the Kahlenberg. The Turkish commander, Kara Mustapha, disagreeing with the advice of his second-in-command Ibrahim, who now that the relieving army was upon them thought that it was time to raise the siege, maintained that the enemy would never be able to advance through the woods of the Wienerwald. He was wrong. At four o'clock on the morning of September 12th the Capuchin monk and Papal Legate said mass on the Kahlenberg on an altar built of drums in the sacristy of the church which had been burnt out by the Turks, and before nightfall the battle had been won and all the rich treasure of the Grand Vizier and of his camp had fallen to the victors, while the Turks fled in a confusion maintained until they reached Raab in Hungary.

The view from this hill carries for an Austrian overtones and associations such as are suggested in Grillparzer's lines where he makes the Kahlenberg, and the green landscape below, the key both to himself and to his writings. On the summit stands now the Josefskirche, dating from 1734, and nearby is the Kahlenberg-Restaurant whose terraces face Vienna. From here the road curving amongst the trees dips and presently rises again until the neighbouring peak of the Leopoldsberg is reached. There the few buildings stand out on the flat summit above the trees, while beyond them and far below lies the vast plain which begins on the far side of the Danube and which stretches away and away over territory that was once part of Austria, towards the Carpathians. For the Leopoldsberg is the last foothill, the last spur of the Alps, which began on the Gulf of Genoa. And its historical significance equals its geographical. For Austria's history may be said to have begun when in 975 a Franconian lord, Leopold of Babenberg, was appointed by the Emperor margrave of the Eastern March and proved himself a stout defender of the Danube valley against the threat of Magyars, Turks and others, and it was a Babenberg who in 1115 built for his wife the castle on the Leopoldsberg—a few years before the family moved down to Vienna—a castle which the Turks destroyed in 1529.

The little church on the summit was rebuilt at the end of the seventeenth century by a Hapsburg Leopold—Leopold I—when the Turkish threat was finally removed, and is dedicated to the memory of a Babenberg Leopold—Leopold III, St. Leopold, known as "The Virtuous"—who built the Abbey of the Augustinian Canons at Klosterneuburg on the spot where his wife's veil, which had blown away years before from the top of the Leopoldsberg, was eventually found.

The Leopoldsberg on a late summer evening is a pleasant spot, with its small tract of green clover and few pines fronting the entrance to the courtyard and with a few lines from the poet

V. O. Ludwig cut in the stone to welcome the visitor to this place and to remind him of its historic past: "O pilgrim of earth whose eye and heart is refreshed here . . ."; and, passing round to the back of the church, the eye is indeed refreshed by the magnificent view down on to the Danube and across the great river to the Bisamberg, behind which stretches league after league of the seemingly endless plain.

From below the northern wall one can look across the tree-tops down to Klosterneuburg which nestles against the foot of the hill and which, seen as a mere matter of roof-tops and spires, does not suggest a town of sixteen thousand inhabitants which since 1938, and despite the ten or twelve miles which separate it from that city, has been constituted the XXVI district of Vienna.

The monasteries of the Danube—Klosterneuburg, Göttweig, Melk and St. Florian, to name the four highlights—are mediæval foundations reborn to considerable architectural magnificence about the time of the three great baroque Emperors, Leopold (d. 1705), Josef I (d. 1711) and Karl VI (d. 1740). To appreciate their significance the visitor really needs to envisage them in a dual light, as part of the Middle Ages, when their political and social importance was very considerable, and when the whole of what is now the province of Lower Austria was a bastion of Christian faith and the final jumping-off ground for the Crusades. But equally, or even more, they must be seen as they were in the hour of their greatest wealth and magnificence, when, the Turk having been defeated and the Counter-Reformation having firmly established itself, the Church, supported by the Imperial Family, indulged in schemes so grandiose that even to-day when the cruel cost of upkeep means that almost all great buildings of this kind have fallen upon evil days, the mere suggestion of their past splendour can still leave us breathless. In the archives of the Vienna Library is an engraving of the lay-out as originally planned by Lucas von Hildebrandt for the Abbey of Göttweig, which suggests not a monastery or a cathedral so much as a battlemented city or a palace of kings. Even the monastic orders of Tibet never planned for such numbers, or, of course, on anything like so impressive a scale. The monasteries drew their

25   GÖTTWEIG: The Main Staircase (1738)
Lucas von Hildebrandt, architect

26 ALTENBURG: A figure in t
Monastery Chapel (c. 1740)

27 ST. PÖLTEN: An angel in tl
Franziskanerkirche

wealth from the wine-growing lands which adjoined them, from Imperial favour and to some extent doubtless from the gifts of the devout. They were a part of the social structure of their time, costing no more, say, than a warren of bureaucrats does to-day, and, very possibly, with a far higher idea of service, although the splendour of their surroundings suggests a touch of rather human pride employed in the furtherance of the affairs of *Le Bon Dieu*. Perhaps the monks reasoned that if earthly kings deserved such state as they were then enjoying the Almighty deserved it a thousand times more.

Klosterneuburg, built originally for the Augustinians in not very satisfactory twelfth-century Gothic, and rebuilt in its present form at the beginning of the eighteenth century, still has its Gothic cloisters beside the church. The Emperor Karl VI decided in 1730 to enlarge the Abbey into what would have been both an Imperial residence and a monastery, like the Escorial in Spain; but of the four courtyards which he planned three were never even begun, although there is still plenty to impress in what was actually achieved. Kornhäusel as late as 1842 completed it. The Neue Bau (New Building) which adjoins the Abbey Church, whose superb choirstalls have immediately above them Matthias Steinl's glass-covered oratory for the Emperor, is worth seeing for its staircase, marble saloon and suite of tapestry-hung rooms. And the St. Leopold's Chapel, which was the chapter-house of the romanesque abbey and the burial place of Leopold III and his family, and was adapted in the baroque manner in 1677, has not only an exquisitely wrought iron screen, but contains one of Austria's greatest art treasures, the enamel altar by Nicolas of Verdun dating from 1181, backed by a painting on wood dating from 1329 which is one of the earliest examples of its kind.

It was the Imperial engineer, the Milanese Donato Felice d'Allio, who drew up the plan for rebuilding the abbey, the east façade of which was to symbolise the idea of secular Imperial might, the west that of divine power. On one of the two great domes rests a wrought-iron version of the Austrian ducal coronet, the original having been entrusted to the keeping of the monastery by the Emperor Maximilian. On the other, the western dome, is the German Imperial crown. Both the monastery library, with its illuminated manuscripts, and the monastery museum, with its objects of ivory, portable altars and Italian bronzes, should be seen.

One does not need to be interested in mediæval abbeys and their contents in order to take delight in the Wachau, that romantic stretch of the Danube valley which reaches as far as Melk, a country of rolling meadows, crops, and vineyards, alternating with fir-clad hills and steep rocky slopes which abut right on the river itself. The whole district gives the impression of romance, charm, fertility and varied interest. Here the landed farmer is the man who counts. As Marboe puts it, "Theirs is the world in all its essence—ploughland, meadows, forest. Black-trunked, heavily grown peartrees stand before the farms, in gardens, in hedges. The peasant dialect is soft, easy-going, manly and kindly." Out in the fields in the outskirts of some village may stand a curious little tower like a tiny minaret. From its summit, reached by a ladder, warning goes forth and directions to helpers, in the case of fire in some outlying farm on the plain beyond. The soil is fertile; vines, apricots which will be used to make brandy, pears, apples, as well as root crops and corn show their appreciation of it; and as in France the farm labourer moves with an air of solid assurance. This landscape still belongs to him rather than to the cars which speed swiftly through it.

Anyone who would like to get away from the more accepted aspects of Austria should shoulder a rucksack, don strong boots and explore the Wachau, which is at its most beautiful in spring, the time of the fruit blossom, or in early autumn. He can work up the river from Klosterneuburg, or can go to Melk and work back down the Danube towards Vienna; and if he is capable at all of taking pleasure in the life of a countryside his heart will very quickly be won. There is nothing monotonous about the Wachau. He will find rolling country and wide plain and tree-laden hills, rising sometimes as high as 3,000 feet; and, always, that air of gracious prosperity which is so reassuring to the unquiet human mind. In short his mood before long will be the mood of holiday.

If his curiosity extends beyond scenery and crops there is plenty to excite it. For this is a country of mediæval castles

whose crag-set ruins still dominate the landscape. Once they held
the line of the Danube or served to control the traffic upon it, or
even—as in the case of the occupants of the dreaded castle
Aggstein, perched upon its giddy eminence above the river (36)
—to levy unlawful tribute, halting their victim by means of a
chain stretched across the great river. The pilgrim was made to
feel that he owed the—relative—safety of this river-route to the
existence of these castles and toll was exacted from him. Three
Crusades passed this way. In 1096 two thousand craft carrying
on board as many as forty thousand crusaders bound for Palestine
passed down the Danube.

If time is a consideration one is probably best advised to drive
to Melk via St. Pölten, cross the river there and then work back
downstream, recrossing it when Göttweig on top of its hill
comes into view. Do not listen to those who might hurry you
past St. Pölten on the ground that with Melk and Göttweig
awaiting you there is no time to be lost. In my opinion there is
no church interior in all Austria which gives a more breathtaking
impression of the merits of rococo sculpture at its—admittedly
infrequent—best than the church of the Franciscans in St.
Pölten. Here, as in some of the figures at Einsiedeln, we have a
delight in the instinctive grace of the human form caught up into
the third heaven of an angelic inspiration, so that what might
have seemed pagan and sensuous achieves instead an innocence
and at the same time an ebullience which is almost unique in the
annals of art. These lovely gilded figures, exquisitely tender, as
in the case of the angel supporting the figure of Our Lord above
the pulpit, are an expression of the deepest feeling for the plastic
beauty of human limbs and of human gesture (27). A sculpture
which attempted the same kind of thing to-day would be dubbed
luscious and sentimental, so tyrannous is the hand which art
fashion lays upon us, so that in the war of rival tendencies we
find it almost impossible to admire opposites unless we meet
them in an entirely different historical context. But in this
church interior, ablaze with the gold of numerous figures, each
figure is like a separate stanza in a sculptural poem whose beauty
overwhelms us. There is nothing unhallowed about it. It is all as
chaste as the ineffable gesture of some dancer in *Les Sylphides*

who too, as she moves across the stage, seems to reflect a value which is almost not of this earth. So the rococo on these rare occasions when it combines an essential innocence of vision with a sensitive and acute awareness of plastic beauty of form seems to offer us the best of both worlds, the earthly and the heavenly. It is no accident that this sculptural art delights in the theme of childhood and makes full use of it; for the child is the symbol of the sanctification of the carnal and the holiness not only of parenthood but of conjugal love. In the rococo, at its best, art attempted and achieved something which has never been done in quite the same spirit either before or since. Time, who refuses to put up his caravan even for one day, seems where art is concerned sedulously averse to take the same treasure out of the caravan twice; unless we like to parallel the rococo by certain Græco-Roman work which to me is of considerably less validity.

If the interior of St. Pölten is lyrical in the extreme there is something epical about the monastery at Melk, which is more like a mighty fortress than a Benedictine abbey, being the largest in all the German lands (28). The huge building extends back at immense length at right angles to the river bank, but its significant feature is the church with its twin towers and mighty cupola which is set back a little between the two lateral wings of the monastery, allowing for an open circular terrace and colonnade immediately in front. The partly hidden façade of the church rises immediately behind this terrace which rises out of the living rock, and below it and a little to the side cluster a few picturesque houses with just room for the white road between them and the river. Melk is a dramatic sight from any angle but most of all from slightly upstream with not only the façade of its church showing but with some indication of the great length of the nearer wing of the monastery.

Melk is the "Medelicke" of the Nibelungenlied. In 985 Leopold I of Babenberg built a castle here and founded an abbey which was taken over by the Benedictines in 1089. The present baroque building was commissioned by abbot Berthold Dietmayr in 1702, who had a good deal to say to the form which it took. The architect was Jacob Prandtauer (1660–1726). He was from

28　MELK: The Abbey (begun in 1701) and the Danube
Jakob Prandtauer, architect

29 The interior,
and (*below*)

30 A wing of the
Library (*c.* 1716)

*Jakob Prandtauer,
architect*

31 GÖTTWEIG: The
baroque Monastery
Church, with its uncom-
pleted towers

32 DÜRNSTEIN: The
main portal of the
Monastery

M. Steinl, architect

33 SCHÖNBÜHEL CASTLE (1820) on its cliff above the Danube

St. Pölten, "a local practitioner", as Sacheverell Sitwell puts it, "with the most grandiose of talents", and he created a building which is marvellously part of the surrounding landscape. The monastery possesses a portrait of Prandtauer and you can see him wearing a white stock and a grey military frock coat with huge buttons and huge cuffs, his right hand resting on a scroll. To stand at the end of the Kaiser Corridor, which is 196 metres long, and look down that white and silent receding vista, brings home to one the scale of the communities which once lived here. The immense church, with its firmly embellished organ-loft, is to me, despite all the praise it has had, a little forbidding and not to be compared with the glories of St. Pölten. The galleried library, with its 80,000 volumes and Pöbel's symbolic figures of the four faculties, Natural Science, Philosophy, Law and Medicine, is impressive (29), but I am happier outside enjoying the architectural calm of the Prelates' Courtyard, which is finely conceived and nobly executed.

In a simple wine cellar with rough-hewn tables and gravelled floor and with a crucifix presiding behind the bar the pilgrim to Melk can drink the monastery wine and eat the food which he has brought with him, before passing out again through the archway into the sunlight. Melk's Post House is a charming classicistic building by an unknown architect. It was built in 1790 and we owe it to the wealthy squire Josef von Fürnberg.

When on April 21st, 1770, Marie Antoinette left Austria to go to France to marry the Dauphin, Joseph II accompanied his sister on her journey as far as Melk and said goodbye to her there. She had been helped, half-fainting, into her carriage earlier in the day at the Hofburg. Both she and her mother realised that they would never meet again, and the latter, taking the sobbing princess in her arms, had whispered to her, "Be so good to the French that they can say I have sent them an angel."

The Danube flows serenely past beneath the great abbey. It is not the Blue Danube, here or anywhere for that matter, except on some rarest occasion generally in late September when, freed from inundation by storms or melting snows, the water becomes limpid and the river is able for an hour or two to reflect the blue of the azure sky overhead. Normally the Danube is brown, opaque, muddy, a contrast to the Rhône, which has deposited its sediment for the most part in a great lake.

A trip downstream by river steamer from Melk is a restful experience. Or one can cross the river on a huge floating barge capable of taking two or three charabancs and as many cars, and drive through the Wachau along the opposite shore. This great ferry—like the smaller passenger ferries at Basel in Switzerland —makes the current of the river do all its work for it. The force of the swiftly flowing water drifts it across, attached to a cable, until it reaches the opposite bank, no mean force indeed to move at right angles to itself what it does.

But before crossing the river one should visit the castle of Schallaburg, which is three and a half miles to the south-east of Melk on a hill approached from the south side. Between 1572 and 1600 the mediæval castle was transformed into one of the most magnificent Renaissance complexes in Lower Austria. The courtyard, with its two storeys of arcades and its terracotta reliefs depicting scenes from Greek myths, is a masterpiece of German Renaissance. Downstream from Melk and on the same side of the river Castle Schönbühel rises from a rocky buttress not unlike that on which the monastery itself is built (33). It is a picturesque sight, with its square tower topped by a small "onion" dome, springing directly from its steep-eaved roof, a prolongation of the façade, and a daring one. The castle was built early in the nineteenth century on the ruins of a twelfth-century structure, and has an air of distinction. In the parish church at Mauer-bei-Melk is a carved altar of the Madonna in glory, with lost souls entreating her aid, which is one of those rare works which illustrate the transition period between Gothic and Renaissance.

The villages of the Wachau are charming and, as one comes to each of them in turn, are their own best introduction. Villages like Schwallenbach or St. Michael with its old fortified church are undisturbed; and as one moves down the bank of the Danube from Emmersdorf opposite Melk one reaches presently the market village of Spitz, built round the vine-clad Tausendeinerberg and within three hours' walking distance of that picturesque and partly wooded plateau the Jauerling. Ahead, and round a rather sharp bend in the river where the Danube turns south and then once more inclines north, lie first Dürnstein (35) and then Stein and its near neighbour Krems.

To the English Dürnstein is bound to possess a unique interest, for it is here that Duke Leopold of Austria imprisoned the Lion Heart until after much bargaining he handed him over to the German Emperor. Vienna is said to have owed its walls to the duke's share of the ransom, but the duke, despite his title of "the Virtuous", was excommunicated by the Pope for interfering with a Crusader. This sunny village on the river's edge, backed by a steep crag on which the ruins of the mediæval castle stand out, was the scene of the exile of the impulsive English king, which stirred us so much when we were children at school, but seems a shade less nostalgic now. This is not the complete end of the world as it seemed to us then. And the hot-tempered Angevin king, it should be remembered, was there thanks largely to his own indiscretions. After the fall of Acre, passing through the streets of the city, he had noticed an unfamiliar banner floating from one of the towers and had asked whose it was. He learnt that it was the banner of Duke Leopold of Austria who had taken the tower. Richard ordered it to be pulled down and trampled in the mire, and added a few words of direct insult to its owner. This was indiscretion one. Indiscretion two was to land at Ragusa—because of a plethora of other enemies elsewhere—on his way from the Holy Land and to attempt to pass through the duke's territories disguised as a merchant. This was asking for trouble. Indiscretion three was to stay at a little inn outside Vienna and allow his page to go into the town in search of food with his—the king's—gloves stuck in his belt. In a life full of mingled indiscretions—of courage, of hot temper and of folly—these were mere trifles, but they proved costly ones.

Did Blondel really make his way to Dürnstein? Did he, in the ancient *langue d'oc*, sing beneath these walls, to which you can laboriously mount in the sunshine of a summer afternoon:

> Donna, vos beautas
> Elas bellas faissos . . .

and hear to the tinkle of his harp a responding bass:

> Si bel trop affansia
> Ta, de vos, non partrai . . .?

It was seventy years later that a French minstrel gave the story literary shape. Undoubtedly England was anxious to learn the whereabouts of her missing king. Blondel de Nesle was a *trouveur* of distinction, was Richard's contemporary, but if he found him at Dürnstein he must have set out with speed from England, for the king was moved to another prison as soon as negotiations with the Emperor were complete. If you are a stickler for historical accuracy you will view with some slight distrust the pleasant Gasthof zum Sanger Blondel in the village with its bunches of green grapes hanging from the wall, and will plump for the nearby and even more charming Gasthof Thiery zum Richard Löwenherz, whose credentials are above suspicion (for the king was undoubtedly, as the Irish would say, "in the vicinity") and whose host has the most excellent taste both in furniture and in cooking.

Dürns ein never grew beyond its mediæval walls, some remnants of which are still standing. It has been described as the loveliest village in the whole Wachau. The mid-fourteenth-century church of the Poor Clares is a vast ruin; but the parish church nearby, once the church of an Augustinian abbey which was founded in 1410 and suppressed in 1788, has one of the finest baroque towers in Austria, and the interior of the church is full of interest. The portal of the church in the abbey courtyard is a most lovely piece of work, the fruit of a collaboration between the sculptor Matthias Steinl, who only took up architecture when he was seventy-eight, and Joseph Mungenast (34). The Irishman St. Columba was hanged at Dürnstein as a suspected spy when he came there as a pilgrim on his way to the Holy Land. But to-day the village hangs no one and is exceedingly popular with actors and painters who come there either to rest or to work.

The Dürnstein parish church has some fine altar paintings by "Kremser Schmidt". Stein, a little further down the Danube, was his birthplace, and Krems, beyond that again, the scene of

34   DÜRNSTEIN: The gate of the Stiftshof and the Monastery Tower
J. Mungenast and M. Steinl, architects

35   DÜRNSTEIN, on a crag above the town

36   The twelfth-century ruins of AGGSTEIN

CASTLES OF THE DANUBE

much of his activity and of a recent and very successful memorial
exhibition of the painter's work, given in the Minoritenkirche
which had fallen on evil days and at one time been a storehouse
for tobacco. There are several lovely drawings by Schmidt in the
Albertina, notably one of a hand; but in this exhibition of a
rather varied talent it was the cartoons drawn on the grey
Lenten church altar cloths which excited me most.

Krems is an ideal place in which to see one of the autumn
wine-harvest processions of the Wachau, when, on Sunday
afternoon, for perhaps the best part of an hour, the various
aspects of rural life and of the vineyards in particular are staged
by families and by groups from the different farms, either on
lorries or horse-drawn vehicles or on foot. Bands play. I have
watched a white goat enthroned in a manure cart solemnly
preceding a most vigorous brass band in full blast. The farms vie
with one another in dramatic presentation. Old-fashioned
costumes are worn. One may see even a knight in armour.
Youths wear the old-fashioned black hats and girls appear in
"dirndl dress", original as well as modern variants. Strictly
speaking one should not refer to an article of clothing as a
"dirndl", as I am sure I have heard English people do. A *dirndl*
is a peasant's daughter, just as his son is a *bua*. What was the girl
is used now to describe the girl's clothing. These are the people
who clink glasses in gay pantomime at some table set high on
a farm cart as the procession goes by, an occasion of real
festival, for there are at least twenty participants for every one
spectator.

In high mediæval times Krems was regarded as the first town
in the land. The Babenberg princes minted their coins here in
1130 and its three churches, the late Gothic citizens' hospital
church, the parish church of St. Vitus, rebuilt by Cipriano
Biasino (1616–30), which is one of the earliest baroque buildings
in Austria, and the fifteenth-century parish church, Church of
Our Lady, rise one above the other amid vine-terraces which
encroach upon the town.

Before ever one reaches Krems one can look across the river
and see the Benedictine abbey of Göttweig stretching along the
flat top of the hill which it monopolises, and visible above the

trees which clothe its flanks. It is silhouetted against the sky, rising amidst lovely rolling country, above the orchards, above the wooded slopes, above the green fields in which we can see white oxen drawing carts laden with great bundles of cut clover. We cross the river, turn inland and shortly find ourselves mounting a winding road amidst trees with Stations of the Cross in shrines at intervals along it.

In 1719, after a disastrous fire, Abbot Gottfried began a magnificent new building in the baroque style to plans by Lucas von Hildebrandt. Sitwell calls Melk and Göttweig "two of the finest conscious buildings in Europe". I take it he means that they claim the eye of the spectator as their natural right, and this is true. But if he had used the word in its everyday significance I would be inclined to say that Göttweig must be not only conscious but pathetically self-conscious to-day of its past splendour. In this age so inimical to great buildings, when we are told that it will take five million pounds to put the palace of Versailles with its twenty-seven acres of roofing back into repair, can a devout millionaire be found to do the same for Göttweig? Or must it decay, as it began to do when it was closed in 1939 by order of the same individual who shouted himself hoarse from the colonnade of the Hofburg, only the prelude to further vicissitudes from the results of which a handful of elderly priests can hardly be expected now to rescue it. Göttweig is impressive, though perhaps not so impressive as Melk. Hildebrandt was asked to incorporate the sixteenth- and seventeenth-century renovated abbey church into his plans, and after his death in 1750 the twin-towered façade was given columns and a classicistic form (31). In the vast hall of the abbey the superb staircase, which was to have been only the northern one of two, is an emblem of a past which seems unlikely to return (25). From the windows of the library one looks down on a small orchard and then across the tree-tops to that green countryside over whose labours the monks once presided.

The Wachau is beautiful with its vineyards, its fields and its gentle wooded gradients. But there are other districts further afield, in Lower Austria, where the traveller can find almost as much to please him. Waidhofen, basking in the sunshine on the upper course of the Ibbs; Amstetten, further down the same river; and Seittenstetten with its restful and dignified abbey courtyard: all lie to the extreme east of the province. The Danube divides Lower Austria from west to east, and roughly speaking, the half to the south of the river is divided by the Wienerwald, and that to the north of it on a line which runs through the Manhartsberg. The north-western quarter need not detain us long. It is a high tableland, falling steeply to the east and south, and is an extension of the old granitic structure of the Bohemian plateau and its southern rim, the Bohemian forest. The soil is poor, the climate rough and the forests are extensive. In consistently good weather a walk through the Waldviertel might be pleasant enough, and Rappottenstein Castle with its five gateways, or Heidenreichstein, that forbidding yet impressive structure, the finest existing example of a mediæval moated castle in Austria, would add interest to it. Then one might turn south to Zwettl, where the Cistercian abbey founded in 1138 has much to show of merit from the Romanesque, Gothic and Baroque periods. The façade of its church, which, being at the bottom of the valley, had to be high in order to be widely visible, was brilliantly conceived by Steinl, and was supervised and completed by Mungenast in the grey granite of the Waldviertel in the five years between 1722 and 1727. In it plastic and architectural invention are finely combined.

Life is easier, yet not so very easy even then, east of the Manhartsberg and the well-loved Hutberg. When the vines are threatened by frost in winter the peasant must light fires whose smoke may help to keep it at bay. The district keeps its old manner of speech and its ancient customs. Marriage celebrations are as elaborate and picturesque as those in Brittany. Life has its rituals: the Kirtag (church festival), the dance of the wine-harvest, the dehusking of the grain (*Weizauslösen*) or the stripping of feathers for down (*Federnschleissen*). The wine-press is often built against the mountainside, below the chestnuts and limes, and reached by a flight of steps and skirted by acacia and elder-berry. As the dark wine-press creaks and groans a hand-pump draws off the fumes which can, and often do, render the labourers unconscious.

From Krems one can go to Horn and from Horn it is only a matter of three or four miles to the village and the Benedictine abbey of Altenburg (26), a building that has had many deserved superlatives ranging from those of Tietze—"It has the richest series of luxuriant stucco decorations handed down to us by the eighteenth century, while the library is the most magnificent and the crypt the most striking room in any Austrian convent"—to those of Sacheverell Sitwell—"If it were better known, the library here would be more famous than the library of Melk, or than the Hof-Bibliothek." Even for persons whose curiosity has been stimulated by phrases such as these, the beautifully spacious monastery library, in its three domed rooms and with its two brooding sphinxes and its two prancing horses helping, in an adjacency which remains mysterious, to support its painted ceiling, is unlikely to prove an anticlimax. Mungenast, who built Dürnstein's church, was responsible with Wisgrill for the abbey, and its paintings, by Paul Troger, are evidence of a genuine feeling for the medium of fresco.

Also accessible from Krems, but lying almost due south of the Danube instead of due north, is Lilienfeld, where will be found another abbey, Cistercian this time, with a mediæval portal which was left untouched in the west façade of its church when the church was rebuilt in 1703. It is less interesting, however, than the amazing thirteenth-century west portal of the parish church at Tulln, which, whatever its debt to upper Italian portals, probably owes still more to an incorporation of late Roman tombstones; for Tulln long before it became the temporary scene of the Babenbergs had been the ancient Commigena, and various Roman regiments were stationed there.

Heiligenkreuz, with its still more famous Cistercian abbey and its romanesque abbey church, lies south of Vienna and, like Baden, with its sulphur springs—which you can smell even on the bridges over the Schwechat—and its memories of Beethoven, Grillparzer, Schubert and other famous men, carries us off on a long journey across the centuries. So does Wiener-Neustadt in the same part of the province, where beneath a window in the west façade of St. George's Chapel you will meet the stone effigy of the Emperor Frederick III surrounded by the fourteen coats-of-arms of the Hapsburg lands, while above are ninety-three heraldic panels containing imaginary coats-of-arms of a legendary princely house, supposed to have ruled Austria from 810 years after the flood until 883 A.D.!

The country around is not particularly inspiring, but the railway which traverses it presently begins climbing; the engine, which may be attached to carriages on their way to Trieste, Venice and Rome, invokes the assistance of a relative, and passengers are drawn slowly onward, up through the pines, towards the Semmering Gorge, till Semmering is reached, a spot well loved by visitors from all over the world, and well deserving to be loved, for its great hotels, like the Sudbahn Hotel, hide themselves at a dignified distance from one another amongst the pines, and, if one deserts for a few hours the very real attractions of their cuisines, one can take a walk in the woods, breathe the resinous scent of the pines, and find oneself as far from the rest of mankind as city-dwellers in the occasional sanity of their hearts could wish to be. In winter Semmering offers good winter sport and is easily reached from Vienna.

V

Burgenland and Styria

THOUGH I have given it precedence Burgenland must be content with a mere paragraph. The average visitor is unlikely to find time for it, and there are various difficulties even if he should wish to include it in his itinerary. It is Austria's youngest province. Until the treaty of St. Germain it was actually a part of the kingdom of Hungary, although its great estates produced much of the food for Vienna; and its nobles—in particular the Esterhazy family—were patrons of art and music and contributed greatly to the cultural life of the Austrian capital. Eisenstadt, the capital of the province, is only forty miles from Vienna (37). There you can see the little house in which Haydn, after being put in charge of Prince Esterhazy's band of fourteen players and made conductor in his private chapel, lived for thirty years, making only occasional trips to the Esterhazy palace in Vienna with his patron. Hither Michael Kelly made a special pilgrimage to visit him. It is a small museum now, shared by the composer of *The Creation* with Liszt and with the illustrious daughter of his music copyist, the dancer Fanny Elssler; for Burgenland, though it is bucolic to the core, honours its famous ones. The taste of the Esterhazy family is established not merely in their patronage of the great musician, or by their palace in Eisenstadt, but still more by the lovely Schloss Kittsee, in the extreme north of the province, which was built for a member of the family by an unidentified architect between 1730 and 1740. It is in the style of Vienna high-baroque and its staircase is a masterpiece of straightforward elegance. A very different building in the province, lying not far south of Eisenstadt, is Forchtenstein Castle, which was the only one of all the frontier fortresses and castles not to fall when the Turks ravished the country in 1683. One has only to look at it on its steep hill to feel that there was a certain excuse for this omission on their part. For the rest Burgenland is best thought of in terms of its rolling green countryside, richly productive, deeply loved by its inhabitants, and with its own immemorial customs such as that of putting violets into the oven when a girl baby is born so that she may not get freckles. The vast reedy Neusiedler Lake, which is shallow at all times and has even been known to dry up on occasion, is a paradise for wild fowl, and—for the Burgenland peasant turns everything to good use—the reeds are used for making mats.

The western boundary of this long, narrow province, which at one point is scarcely more than a few kilometres in width, is the eastern limit of Styria, a province nearly ten times its size, of which it has been said that within its 16,000 square kilometres "the traveller may find and enjoy within the short span of one day the climate and geographical formations of an entire continent." Few foreign visitors are ever likely to think of Styria in what might be called strictly provincial terms, for its different parts are far more likely to be crossed into from some adjoining province: Bad Aussee, for example, from Salzburg or the Salzkammergut; Graz after passing through the Semmering Gorge and descending via Bruck; Mariazell from St. Pölten in Lower Austria. One passes into Styria without being aware of it, and slips out again equally unconscious of the debt. Only in a spot like Admont, reached by the slow peregrinations of a provincial railway, is the danger of geographical confusion really kept at bay.

But the inhabitants of the province are stoutly conscious of their separate heritage, and it has been well loved by many persons, including the Archduke Johann, that interesting individual who insisted on the railway line being constructed from Graz to Köflach, drawing up the plans with his own hands, and who made a morganatic marriage with a citizen of the province, Anna Plochl, the postmaster's daughter at Bad Aussee, changing his name to Johann Orth, and sailing the seven seas in his windjammer, the *Santa Margherita,* before disappearing mysteriously and completely from the face of this globe. Styria has not been isolated through the centuries. It is too much in the line of transit for that. Tombstones have been found amongst the woods commemorating in Roman lettering the Celtic natives. The Avars overran the country and it was not until 800 A.D., after Charlemagne had broken their power, that the monks were sent from Salzburg to preach the Christian faith. In the twelfth century the Count of Steyr was given charge of these frontier lands by the Emperor and it is he who has given his name to the province.

The Styrian Alps dominate the whole northern part of the province, running from west to east. Neighbouring the southern and eastern slopes of the Dachstein, that peak nearly 10,000 feet high, where the boundaries of Upper Austria, Salzburg and Styria meet, are the lower peaks of the Kalkalpen—Hochmöbling, Totes Gebirge, Hochtausing, Grimming and Stoderzinken —their shapes nearly as divergent as their names. And on the north-eastern side of the province the Hochschwab group cover an area of 400 square kilometres and number more than a hundred separate peaks. From them one can look north across the Danube to the high-lying Waldviertel, west to the Dachstein and beyond it to the Glockner, and south to the unbroken wall of the Karawanken Alps.

Marboe's *Austria* quotes the attributes of the inhabitants of the different districts: "Dour but gallant the Ennstaler; charming the Ausseer girl; thoughtful and grave the Murbodner; solemn, good trencherman the east Styrian; and all tough and courageous in the cause of the Motherland." My own experience of the Styrian of the high mountain valleys is one of deep and genuine good will, less affable perhaps than the inhabitant of the Tyrol because less accustomed to the stranger, but fundamentally kind of heart.

For those who are always sighing because of difficulty in finding their escape from the beaten track the highlands of Styria might offer the kind of thing they seek. Unlike the Tyrol where the valleys strike out at right angles, north and south of the one main valley of the Inn, a number of valleys here may radiate out from a central cup which is flat and level, and wide enough often to be almost given the name of plain. From a central town or village one can explore in half a dozen different directions. The lower slopes of the mountains are thickly wooded, and Styria is a province where it is not difficult to recollect and to accept the

37   EISENSTADT: A country church near the capital of Burgenland

38   VORAU: The Library of the Monastery, decorated with paintings by Hackhofer

39   *VOITSBERG* on the Mur near Graz

40   MARIA GAIL: Detail of the Altar (1526)

rather astonishing fact that 37·4 per cent. of the total surface of modern Austria is covered by woods, as against the not very much greater figure of 49·3 for farmland.

In the Styrian Alps there is no danger of aspects of peasant life being staged for the mere benefit of the visitor. It is the real thing. These people, although they know much about milking, are not yet aware that the udder of tourism can sometimes be helpfully aided by the mangold-wurzel of deliberately-arranged and picturesque local detail. If they dance they still dance simply and solely to please themselves. If they wear the costume of their valley it is for the same good reason.

Indeed the implied sneer where costume is concerned is unfair, for the Austrian pleasure in national costume, wherever you may go in the country, has little or nothing to do with the intruder. This revived interest—for in the second half of the nineteenth century the traditional costumes seemed likely to receive their death sentence: the railways were carrying women hastening to the towns to purchase hats to replace the customary handkerchief or bonnet, and young men were even abandoning their leather shorts—was due in the first place to a definite movement amongst enthusiasts, and then to a wave of patriotism following upon the trials the country had to endure after the first world war. In adversity men rally to whatever seems a reminder of the past staunchness of their race, as though invoking the shades of their ancestors.

The vagaries of peasant fashion are an interesting theme. Apparently Napoleon's invasion of Austria gave many of the villages a different headgear, and the high waist-line and long, narrow skirt that are still to be seen in certain places originated nearly a century and a half ago in what was then the fashionable Empire cut. In the Vorarlberg women still wear the most delightfully comfortable-looking round fur caps, and these caps according to tradition originated as a fashion after the *débâcle* in the French army in 1809 when members of the Napoleonic guard would throw away their caps and these might be picked up and worn by the women in the villages to mock later arrivals in the general retreat. It is a picturesque story certainly, even if it lacks foundation.

Styria has its folk costume, its folk dances and its folk songs. In his *Steyrisches Raplwerk* Konrad Mautner notes that in a single Styrian village of barely one hundred inhabitants he was able to record over 700 dance songs. It was at Grundlsee in Styria that he found a pithy quatrain which even those who are without acquaintance with the German language should be able to interpret after a fashion:

> Der Adam hat d'Liab auf-bracht,
> D'r Noah n'Wein,
> Und der David das Zither-schlag'n
> Müessen Steirer g'west sein.

As well as their dances with the womenfolk, which are compact of spontaneous gaiety and often very charming (for example the *Schuastapolka*, the Shoemakers' Polka, from Upper Styria; or the *Schneckentanz*, the Snails' Dance, also from Styria, where a chain of dancers, holding hands, follow the leader through the whole house), the men have dances of their own, executed at the end of the day's work, as a form of relaxation, to the music of a zither, mouth-organ or guitar. Such is the Styrian *Wischtanz*, where a couple hold an alpenstock, and, to slow waltz time, execute elaborate manœuvres in conjunction with it.

If one approaches Styria from Vienna through the Semmering Gorge the train takes one through a succession of alpine and sub-alpine valleys on the way to Bruck and thence to Graz, which is the capital of the province. It is a slow descent through delightful scenery, mountains, rivers, grey crags on which perch the ancient ruins of some castle, and then a gentler landscape, and one of my personal favourites, rolling alps, partly pasture, partly wooded, and very similar to the country that one sees rising behind Rougemont and Saanen in the Bernese Oberland. On these slopes fawn-coloured cows, light-boned, and not unlike the Jersey cow, graze. If it is autumn the hay hangs drying on great longitudinal racks in the fields or near to the farmhouse. Monster pumpkins laid on some stone step in the yard recall the prodigality of summer, while in the fields girls hoe some late crop or kneel, sorting and heaping the potatoes which their menfolk have dug that morning. Behind rise the pastures and the scented pines.

This sub-alpine scenery always takes us—always takes me personally—to its heart. Of all European landscapes it is the most Arcadian; in fact it is very much what you will find if you go to Arcady in Greece. What is it that makes it so congenial? It is something more than sunshine and clean mountain air. Is it perhaps the subtle suggestion, which is undoubtedly always present, that man and Nature have here come to satisfactory terms, that the world and all its dirty tricks are at a safe distance, and that for those with staunch hearts Nature, though she can be terrible, is in the main kindly disposed? Sit in the sun for a minute and listen. No sound comes to you that does not carry with it the implications of age-old continuity. Scene and mode of life are unperturbed and unperturbable. Man has struck a bargain with the seasons and the elements, and so long as he keeps it, does not demand too much, and does not idle, they will assure him his modest share of happiness.

At Bruck the railway branches. One line goes to Graz, while the other (joined before long by a branch line which has come from Selzthal and which links up not only with Bad Gastein and Bischofshofen but, via Steinach, with Bad Aussee, Bad Ischl and the Salzkammergut) continues on its way to Klagenfurt and Villach in Carinthia. Bruck, it will be seen, is therefore a place from which a number of topographical decisions may be made, and perhaps having seen the Kornmesser House with its arcades and loggia, probably the finest of all late Gothic houses in Austria (41), as well as the wonderful wrought-iron Market Fountain which directly faces it, one should take the opportunity of its relative adjacency and take a morning to go and have a look at the Erzberg. The Iron Mountain is 2,400 feet high, and it has been turned into a veritable step pyramid, of nearly sixty steps, each forty feet high, by the surface excavations of miners. The ore has been worked since the time of the Romans. Styria is called the Iron Province and the Erzberg alone is enough to make it a rich one. Legend relates that a merman captured in the Leopoldsteinersee offered mountain treasure to the natives if he were set free, gold for one year, silver for ten or iron for ever.

They chose iron and their descendants have had no reason to regret their choice.

Graz, the capital of Styria, is the second largest town in Austria, and, with its iron, linen, hat, leather and paper works, its breweries and its mills, may not seem to hold forth the happiest prospects to a tourist. Its situation is highly favourable, for it bestrides the Mur at a spot where the river leaves a narrow defile and enters the long stretch of the fertile *Grazer Feld*. If we over-look certain aspects of its industrialisation, which are confined mainly to the right bank, the town has still plenty that is lovely and picturesque to offer a visitor. Much of the river frontage is dignified and has great charm, and the Schlossberg and its famous adjoining belfry standing upon a wooded height above the river is the sort of landmark that is not easily forgotten.

Graz has a long history, ranging from prehistoric times when its site was already occupied, to Babenberg times and the thirteenth century when it received walls, and on to the fifteenth century when Frederick III gave it its artistic importance, and the sixteenth when it became the residence of the Styrian line of the Hapsburgs. Architecturally the town is a mixture of late Gothic, Lombardian Renaissance and Italian early Baroque. I shall not venture an opinion on the Mausoleum which Ferdinand II had designed, adjoining the cathedral, as the place of his tomb and a triumphant reminder of the victory of the Counter-Reformation —"a showy baroque edifice" according to one authority, "a classic example of Mannerist architecture", with its fluid and perfectly controlled balance of parts, in the eyes of another. I shall merely say that to me its façade is an illustration of how baroque can be not only wildly exciting but also deadly dull. Perhaps "the wretched Ferdinand", as Crankshaw calls him, did not deserve anything better in the way of a memorial. "The whole of his reign", the latter says, "was shadowed by that fearful reversion to barbarity which historians have dignified with the name of The Thirty Years' War. . . . Ferdinand, with his barbaric but astonishingly able general, Tilly, became a sort of demoniac scourge of Central Europe and a death's-head to its struggling culture. Sweeping all before him in a fantastic cam-paign of bigotry and greed, its sordidness relieved by a solitary gleam of romance in the personality of his second general of genius, Wallenstein, at one time it seemed that Protestantism would be utterly wiped out of Europe and the Hapsburg hegemony secured from the Adriatic to the Baltic . . . the hero of this war is Gustavus Adolphus, the Protestant king of Denmark (*sic*), who, roused at length to action by the shrill hysteria of Ferdinand, rose with deliberation and advanced slowly and with the invulnerable momentum of a steam-roller, towards the south; and although at Lützen he was killed, he had Leipzig behind him and Lützen itself was won, and Hapsburg had shot its bolt.''

This is an occasion on which one is left in no doubt as to where a writer's sympathies lie. I enjoy vigorous polemics, even if they seem to need some qualification. Mr. Crankshaw's onslaught, a few pages before, upon the eccentric Emperor Rudolph, to whose connoisseurship we owe some of Austria's greatest art treasures, is almost as severe, but I can forgive some misanthropy and eccentricity in the man who purchased so many of those masterpieces which, at the moment when I write, are on tour in America and delighting the Americans.

Graz's cathedral, with Schoy's altar, the fine frontage of the Mariahilfe Kirche, built in the Italian style by Pietro de Pomis, 1607–11, the Mausoleum, the armoury with its interesting portal, the Renaissance Landhaus, the Schlossberg and Graz's fine museum, which throws much light on the history and the customs of the province, will all engage our attention, and pottering about the town our imagination may furnish us with flash-backs of certain famous figures. Kepler taught mathematics in Graz from 1594 to 1600. Of nearer interest to me is a certain moody schoolboy, sent to Graz by his father, a leather merchant reduced to poverty by a fire in 1867, who had the distress of seeing him expelled from three schools before he was sixteen. After this disquieting beginning Hugo Wolf persuaded his family to let him go to Vienna to study music at the Konservatorium. There he bearded Wagner in his hotel—a considerable achievement for anyone, much less a student with no greater backing than that of a compassionate chambermaid—wrote off Cosima as ''an exceedingly haughty and conceited lady'', and actually heard the hero of his dreams say to him, ''I wish you, dear friend, much fortune in your career.'' It is all set down in one of those letters which passed between Vienna and Windischgraz, from son to father. They loved each other well, those two: the nagged, neurotic, misanthropic father who, when a mad dog ran through the streets and forty dogs had to be destroyed, wrote to Vienna: ''But what is *hydrophobia* compared to the ravings of a wife?''; and the equally neurotic, violently-tempered son, who would no sooner get a job at Salzburg than he would lose it, yet who, despite the miseries and uncertainties of his life, could write: ''Dearest Father! Your melancholy letter has really alarmed me. Who is going to despair like that straight away? Courage! Courage! We will present a brow of iron to all afflictions.'' Out of it all—elation alternating with misery—would come one day the immensely nostalgic and subtle nuances of the *Mörike-Lieder*; but the father would be dead and the son would exclaim, ''Ah, why do I go on composing when he can no longer hear?—he, who only in music lived and breathed, and for whom *my* music never sounded, to whom my song never spoke!''

The visitor to Styria who finds time to make his way to Pollau to see the church of the former Augustinian abbey there, with its rather pleasing late eighteenth-century outer building; or to Wolfsberg, at the heart of the Lavanttal, with its attractive square (47); or to Vorau where are the early west façade of the Monastery of the Prebendaries and its baroque library, which is a smaller and more modest version of the kind of thing that the great libraries of the period attempt, will not feel unrewarded (38). More imperative, however, are Mariazell and Admont, neither of them particularly accessible, but both of them deserving his attention. He can go from Bruck to Mariazell by Alpine post car, the road ascending slowly until it reaches this, the most famous pilgrimage shrine in Austria, which is said to stand on the spot where the twelfth-century monk, carrying an ikon carved out of the wood of the lime tree, sank exhausted before an impassable wall of rock which in answer to prayer parted and showed him a way of escape to the valley below. The Gnaden-Kirche stands in the middle of the Haupt-Platz, and its three western towers, the central one Gothic, the other two with baroque onion-shaped tops, dominate this pleasant market village. Within the church will be found the Knaden-Kapelle, where behind a silver railing is the miracle-working limewood image of the Virgin. Women and girls who wear its emblem about their necks are protected from evil and promised charm and cheerfulness to help them on their way through this earthly pilgrimage. Mariazell is not only a place of pilgrimage, known, like Einsiedeln, all over the world, but an agreeable summer resort, and in winter visitors come here for winter sports.

From Bruck one can get to Admont by rail, either by Eisenerz or by Donawitz, St. Michael and Selzthal. The latter a hundred years ago was not even a village but the mere name of a district. Now, in the centre of its valley, with railway lines branching out from it in four directions, it still keeps an air of the mountains, although its population is over the two-thousand mark. Between Selzthal and Admont both road and railway pass close to the Kulm, a small cone-shaped hill, rising abruptly from the floor of the valley, and flanked by trees, on the summit of which stands dramatically the pilgrimage church of Frauenberg or Maria Kulm. Its adjoining monastery is practically abandoned, but the church is in the loving care of the monks of Admont and it is well worth climbing to it, as I have done, on a late autumn morning to enjoy its baroque splendour, with the choir of angels carved by Stammel, to see its votive paintings and the tray of little wax figures—a man, a woman, a swathed baby, a cow, a horse— which must be still poured into moulds at least two centuries old and which are there for the benefit of the faithful who like to leave a modest coin in their place recording their gratitude for favours vouchsafed. Outside, sunlight fills the valley all round, and a narrow chestnut avenue leads to the hill's edge, over-looking pleasant sloping green fields, where there is a Calvary standing above arcaded vaulting in which great wooden painted figures, carved with peasant naïveté, depict the various types who witnessed the Crucifixion.

Admont—although you will find a swimming bath there for your entertainment in summer, and can ski nearby at a height of 6,000 feet on the Scheiblingstein in winter—is a typical simple north Styrian market village in the centre of the wide, flat valley floor and with delightful views all round, first of low wooded alps and then of higher peaks, granite and often snow-covered. Its famous Benedictine abbey was founded in 1074. The present buildings were designed in 1734 and partly rebuilt after a fire in 1865. Fortunately the library was saved, and the library is worth coming a long way to see. It is huge, but Heyberger has given it a lightness and graciousness of design which prevents one from being over-conscious of the fact. The white and gold bookcases decorated with a fine succession of gilded heads of writers, many of them pagan, add to this general effect of lightness and grace. Above these runs the gallery with more bookcases, and above that again are ceiling paintings by Altomonte amongst others. At the four corners of the central division of the library stand Stammel's famous figures, Death, Judgment, Hell and Heaven, dating from 1760 and carved from limewood. His Death is matchless of its kind and establishes him as the greatest of provincial Austrian sculptors of his time (42). Not a great deal is known of him apart from his work. He had been to Rome, but from about 1725 until his death in 1765 the greater part of his life was spent in the service of the monastery at Admont. In the carving Man appears as a pilgrim with shell and pilgrim's hat, while winged Death overtakes him with hour-glass and dagger. It is an incomparable work of its kind, showing respect for the medium, wood, while at the same time launching itself upon the most daring flight of imagination. In the case of the floating figure of Death it attempts successfully what most carvers would have said was quite impossible. In its extreme and detailed realism it is a complete offshoot from the great tradition of German mediæval woodcarving: nevertheless without that tradition it is inconceivable that it could ever have come to exist.

From Admont we can return to Selzthal and from there, through a succession of wide, pleasant valleys where great beds of tufted rushes, which are scythed in autumn, threaten what looks to be excellent pastureland and to be equally successful in the production of good root crops—and where, instead of great hay barns, innumerable tiny wooden ones, with an entrance under the eaves, for when the snow lies thick on the ground, are dotted everywhere about the fields—the train or the road will take us to

41 BRUCK AN DER MUR: The late
Gothic Corn Measurer's House

42 ADMONT: "Death", from a
series in the Monastery Library
(1760)

Johann Thadäus Stammel, sculptor

43   NEUSIEDL AM SEE with its baroque church

44   The old well at ILLMITZ

45   A country church near GREIFFENBERG

46   A wayside shrine in CARINTHIA

48 GRAZ: The façade of
the church of Maria-hilf
(1607–11)

Steinach, where we can decide whether to continue on our way along the picturesque descent to Bischofshofen in the province of Salzburg or to follow the branch railway line which will take us over the col and on to Bad Aussee.

Since this chapter is on Styria and since Bad Aussee is still in that province, albeit in what is known as the Styrian Salzkammergut, we will here elect for the second alternative. And indeed anyone who does so will have no need to regret it, for, dramatic as the winding descent to Bischofshofen is, the side line on which we have chosen to travel will take us through country as charming, in my opinion, as any in all Austria, the kind of country that makes us feel that we want to get out at the next halt, find a modest room at some nearby chalet, and never again in all our mortal life leave this spot on which God's peace seems so surely to rest.

Leaving Steinach, the perpendicular grey flank of the Grimming, that 7,713-foot giant which from a distance had still dominated the linked succession of level valleys through which we have just come, uprears its bulk immediately on our left. Should we get out on the small deserted station platform at Pürgg we will have a ten minutes' walk up to the picturesque village which looks across to that mountain. Its huge romanesque church, remodelled in Gothic style, has the local name of "Steyrisches Kripperl", Styrian Crib. Nearby is the intensely interesting St. John's Chapel, with frescoes which belong to the Salzburg School and which date from about 1200. The building was probably used as a baptismal chapel and the paintings, which are in a very fair state of preservation, take us right back to another age. They include one of mice besieging a citadel of rats. Church, chapel, inns and farmhouses all press in upon one another in what is really this mountain nest "in der Pürgg".

For some distance the railway line continues to cling to the mountainside on its right, offering striking views of the Grimming across the intervening valley, and reminding one a little of that stretch of the Lötschberg railway in Switzerland soon after Brigue is left. Sometimes one looks down on a sea of green fir tops. A moment later one is crossing a rushing mountain stream. Then the towering grey, fluted sides of the Grimming are left behind, and we enter a pastoral scene as pleasant as any in the whole Alps. Cows graze on gradients which may be steep, but which are more likely to be gentle and to slope up to a small copse of firs or pine trees where some forester is at work. As well as these green alps, across which the cattle move, comes an occasional cultivated field where women and girls are kneeling to save the potato crop. What gives this whole terrain its charm is not the mere variety of the scene, the freshness of the air one breathes and the remoteness of it all from the world, but that same feeling of a partnership between man and nature which I have noted earlier and which may almost be said to set the seal of Arcady upon any highland district which possesses it. Presently the line begins to descend slightly, and at the next halt at the head of a valley as pleasant as any that have gone before, one is surprised to read the name Bad Aussee; for, though still in Styria, we have entered the Salzkammergut almost unawares, and from the least wonted direction. I shall leave this delightful mountain village, as well as the lovely neighbouring lake of Grundlesee, until I return to the Salzkammergut from a wholly different direction in a later chapter.

VI

Carinthia

To the tourist and to those fairy godparents of tourism the travel agencies, Austria tends to reduce itself to the Tyrol, Salzburg, the Salzkammergut and Vienna. Consult them in relation to any of these and their hand has only to reach up and take down the necessary ticket. Nor is the traveller likely to be disappointed in their choice for him, for the popularity of the Tyrol, like the popularity of Switzerland, is well-tried and well-deserved, and a town like Innsbruck can be depended upon to live up to its reputation. Nevertheless it is a fact that some of the most beautiful places and one of the most beautiful provinces in Austria are not included in this list at all. Carinthia is the province that I have in mind, and if the fact that it was made a part of the British zone after the second world war, and that the military command had their headquarters there, has resulted in a certain number of Britishers and a few of their wives becoming acquainted with it, nevertheless the province as a whole still awaits the serious attention of the nation. It lies cupped between two great ranges of mountains, and shaped rather like an empty mussel-shell, in the extreme south of Austria, and although high mountain ranges separate it from each of these countries, it shares borders with both Italy and Jugoslavia. The latter would have liked to deprive it of some of its territory after the first world war and again after the second; but the peasants stood firm in each instance, to the point even of defending themselves with arms in 1919, and a plebiscite decided in their favour.

It will take you a little longer—a negligible amount if you fly, a few hours if you travel by car or train—to reach Carinthia than to get to Salzburg. But those few hours will be amply repaid. By whatever route we arrive, we will either have come to it through a tunnel or descended upon it from a height. This is misleading, however, if the reader envisages a province of steeply enclosed valleys shut in by sheer precipices. Just the reverse is true. Once the centre of the province has been reached we find ourselves in the most delightful sub-alpine territory, starred with lakes which are nearly as beautiful as the Lake of Lucerne and more intimate and unspoilt than the Lake of Zürich, and around which stretch tracts of gentle undulating country varied by wooded heights, all of it of a sort to warm the heart and delight the eye.

I am thinking particularly of the terrain around the Wörthersee when I describe it thus, and perhaps it will be best to jump straight into the province and begin with the Wörthersee, merely noting that to get there you will in all likelihood either have come over the Grossglockner Pass, down to Lienz, and on to Spittal and Villach, or else gone through the tunnel of the Tauern railway from Bad Gastein to Spittal. If, however, you came from the direction of Vienna it will have been via the Semmering Gorge and Bruck, and you will in all likelihood have had a look at Graz on the way.

And now you have reached the Wörthersee and must decide where to reside on the border of that ten-mile-long lake, which varies in breadth from half a mile to a mile, a lake which gives each of its two shores an opportunity of enjoyment in the other. You may prefer to stay at Klagenfurt, whose roofs and steeples can be seen rising at the eastern end. The town from a distance looks as though it might be on the lake itself, but actually it is a little way back from it, linked to it by rail and tram, and by a canal which was constructed as far back as 1527. But the Wörthersee is so lovely that you are more likely to elect for one of the villages actually on its edge. I have known those who gave the palm to Pörtschach, and certainly this village on a flat spur of the north bank, about half-way down the lake, is a most agreeable spot with its hotel and its villas half hidden amongst trees in their green gardens. Behind it the fields rise dotted with farms and more villas but not unduly so.

All the same, pleasant as Pörtschach is, I myself give the palm to Velden at the top end of the lake (50); although I hasten to say that I have never stayed at Velden at the height of its summer season, when, immensely popular as the place is with the Austrians themselves, I am told that its agreeable water frontage is apt to become almost solid with happy bathers. I know nothing

49　A hay barge on the Weissensee

50　Pleasure boats at VELDEN on the Wörthersee

51   GMÜND in Carinthia

about this, just as I know nothing about the St. Moritz of mid-December. Velden is smaller than St. Moritz but it is like it in one agreeable respect, its popularity has, so far, not robbed it of a certain basic simplicity. I believe that this can only happen when the hoteliers and the *commune* steadfastly set themselves against rapid and competitive development. It is thus that beauty spots sell themselves to the devil. St. Moritz, I believe, already has an edict against any further hotels. Velden might be well advised to do the same. Those which it has are excellent. If it wants any more the whole nature of the place must inevitably change.

I have stayed at the Schloss Hotel early in October and, after a week of rain immediately previously in Vienna, have had summer restored fourfold into my bosom by the Velden clerk of the weather. I could cross the road from the castle—for the hotel is a converted nobleman's residence, first built in 1603—with its picturesque four turrets and its delightful garden, and eat my lunch in the sunshine at a table on the terrace, looking down the ten miles of utterly still, serenely blue water, to the far end of the lake and the vaguely suggested Klagenfurt. Narrow wooden jetties, bathing enclosures, diving boards and a long line of dinghies tied one to the other and extending far out into the water suggested the activities of the holiday-makers, just as the splash of a bather brought it nearer still. But Velden actually seemed to have sunk back upon its pleasant and native self. A few weeks before the Princess Royal had stayed here and the village had entertained her with fireworks on the lake and she had written afterwards that nothing could ever make her forget her stay at the Schloss. Now that was all over for the year and, instead of crowds and laughter, one had utter peace, a few late stayers basking in deck-chairs and a local mother taking her children for a very slow row in a very old boat. One or two yachts still swung at anchor, and when the breeze got up and the lakewater began to show ripples, were manœuvred for half an hour or so with extraordinary skill by casually dressed young men who could make a large yacht with an immense mast sail straight up towards the windows of the hotel's waterside restaurant and at the last instant turn at direct right-angles to it. An astonishing pedal boat, consisting of a large platform on torpedo-shaped floats and with three steps descending into the water for convenience of swimmers, was tied up in a tiny harbour of its own. It rejoiced—shades of Watteau—in the name Ile d'Amour, and I would have liked to board it and go for a quiet bicycle ride. But instead I sat there, enjoying the scene, just as I used at night to enjoy the sound of the water slapping against the lakeside. I allowed my eye to travel up the green slopes that rise immediately behind the village to the north, with their patches of woodland, their villas and their still higher farms. I wished that I had my own children with me and could take them for a row like the woman in the boat. Velden seemed the sort of place where a child, let loose before breakfast in the still morning air, to dip an apprehensive toe in the water or to watch a magic shoal of half a dozen small fish flick their tails defiantly round jetty steps, would feel that life was indeed good. That morning I had amused the kind proprietress of the Schloss Hotel before breakfast by rushing excitedly to her and saying, "You must, you simply *must* give me a photograph of God Almighty." Then when she looked a little puzzled by my demand I had added, "It is, isn't it, God Almighty, with the gold triangle above the head, and not just a saint or an angel?" For in the hall of the Schloss itself—I myself was sleeping in the equally comfortable dower-house, or Cavalier House, as it is called, across the garden—I had discovered on the white wall a small masterpiece of painted baroque carving, jettisoned from some church, goodness knows when, to fall into the hands of goodness knows whom, before coming to rest again on this wall. Go and look at it, for it is worth seeing—a bearded figure to about the waist, with the head turned slightly to one side, the hands extended in blessing and the robe lapped across the body and flung back over one shoulder so that its folds float out, as though tempest-blown, behind the head. What long and fine tradition of carving and what individual skill of particular craftsman lies behind this truly lovely thing? For tradition there must be for anyone to carve folds of drapery like that or like the open folds hanging below the wrists, and individual feeling there must have been to give the face with its wind-swept beard its gentle, dreamy, benign and slightly Blakeian expression and to take such obvious delight in the colours of the grey wind-swept beard and the faintly flushed cheeks. The figure breaks off at the waist, where it is supported by a bulging cumulus cloud. Was it part of an Ascension or what? God giving His blessing to Jesus in mid-air? All the colouring is delightful, gold, dove-grey, silver, rose-pink, and the feeling behind every detail of the carving is remarkable. It is an anonymous *chef d'œuvre* come to rest in a corner where I hope many notice it.

Further down the lake, on its south shore, a peninsula, similar to the one at Pörtschach, thrusts out with just room for the group of trees, the two churches and the few buildings which constitute Maria Wörth. Here indeed is a peace with which even Velden in late summer cannot compete. One descends from the main lakeside road, above which the woods are rising, to this demi-isle, which is the kind of spot where it becomes almost eventful to see a sleepy dog turn lazily in the sun and scratch its ear. In other words, serenity broods over Maria Wörth and one is caught into it and made a part of it straight away. The two churches—the Gothic parish church with its double nave, its romanesque crypt and its baroque furnishings, and the small Winter Church which enjoys the alternative name of the Rosenkranz-Kirche and which was rebuilt about 1355 but has a fresco of the apostles dating back to nearly 1130—are within a few yards of one another, which suggests overcrowding; but Maria Wörth could no more seem overcrowded than it could seem hustled or fussed. The churches bask in the sun, and one comes in out of the warm air to explore them on tiptoe and with hushed whispers, for, though there is no one else about, they have laid this measure of their spirit upon us.

The inhabitants of Klagenfurt are inclined to apologise for it, more or less on the lines of "it's quiet down here", as though that needed an apology. But my own impressions of this town, which has been the capital of Carinthia since 1518, are entirely favourable to it. Its streets have a leisurely air, and if Klagenfurt wants to boast of its contribution to progress let it remind us that it was one of its citizens, Emmanuel Herrman, who in 1869 first invented the post-card. Klagenfurt has had a dragon as its seal and symbol ever since the thirteenth century, and in 1590 the sculptor Ulrich Vogelsang hewed an immense dragon out of a single huge stone block for the fountain which the citizens had decided to erect in their square. Forty years later they seem to have grown ashamed of their heraldic device, for Michael Hönel added a Hercules confronting the dragon and about to slay it— dirty work, if not at the cross-roads, then in the square, and perhaps indicative of the same inferiority complex which makes a Klagenfurtian to-day apologise for having no skyscrapers. The dragon has not yet been scotched and you can see it with its jaws opened far apart—not, I believe, so much in any spirit of savagery as in shrill hysterical protest against this base injustice which has been done to it. As well as the wronged dragon there are plenty of interesting old buildings in the town, notably the Landhaus with its two towers and its half-enclosed courtyard with its two-storeyed arcade.

I hesitate to send the reader in search of antiquities which may not interest him, unless there is some concomitant, in the way of attendant scenery, to console him if he should be bored when he gets there. No one who travels up the Danube to Melk, or who visits Göttweig on its spacey hill-top, is going to feel that his time has been entirely wasted. And in the same way, to set out from Klagenfurt and to drive into the heart of the Carinthian country, with Gurk Abbey as our ultimate objective, will be rewarding quite apart from what we may see when we get there, because of what we shall have already seen en route.

One drives out from Klagenfurt, not along the canal side to where it joins the lakeside where people build themselves pleasant summer villas upon piles driven in the marshy ground, but in the opposite direction across an open, extensive and rather pleasant plain—a tiny portion of which is "for ever England", for the British cemetery is there—and although Gurk and its abbey are still a good way distant, before long, so much largesse thrown into our laps, we see perched on its 1,600-foot hill which rises abruptly out of the plain the pilgrimage church of Maria Saal standing in the midst of its fortified graveyard. The temptation will be to rest content with a glance at what is a strikingly dramatic addition to the landscape. But the temptation should be sternly resisted. Even if one is on foot it is worth leaving the main road and trudging the intervening mile and a half to climb the hill. In fact, interesting as Gurk is, I find nearly as much at Maria Saal to excite me. In that rather rambling complex of very ancient buildings, with its arcaded charnel-house (periodically the bones of an Austrian graveyard have to be dug up and deposited in a charnel-house to make room for fresh burials), its church, its two or three adjoining dwelling places, its Volkschule, and its protecting wall and its arched entrance, one is fascinated by a perfect wealth of associations before ever one enters the church at all. For one thing the builders have embedded a number of ancient Roman tombstones in the external walls of the church. The most famous of these is what is known as the Roman Mailcart (54). One would need to be strangely indifferent to history not to be moved at all by this vivid realistic relief, the two horses forging forward, the Roman driver with his whip upraised holding the reins with a professional skill the evidence of which not even nearly two thousand years of weathering have been able to obliterate from the rough stone; and then the covered wagon with its window through which one passenger peers timidly forth. The driven rain must still beat against this relief, as it has been doing for so many centuries; but it has been given a little protection from above by a narrow drip-board, an attention still refused to its almost equally interesting neighbour on the same wall, a relief which depicts Achilles dragging the body of Hector behind his chariot around the walls of Troy. The fifteenth-century marble Keutshach tombstone, which amongst a number of others is also set in the wall of the church, is a lovely piece of work, but I find the Roman survival the more interesting, perhaps because that mailcart has driven so far across the years. Within the church one finds a wealth of interest too, mediæval tombs, fifteenth-century wall paintings, baroque carvings multitudinous, including a fine organ-loft and a saint finely depicted amongst clouds and many cherubs against one of the pillars on the right. Altogether Maria Saal is, in the appropriate cliché, "not to be missed".

We continue upon our way along a straight road between poplars newly-planted. Presently we see Tanzenburg monastery perched on its hill across the valley; and now we pass the Herzog-Stuhl or ducal chair, a seat by the roadside, made from Roman inscribed stones. From it, until 1597, the Dukes of Carinthia awarded their fiefs. As we near St. Veit, which our road will just skirt, we shall have to decide whether to turn aside and see that town where Walther von der Vogelweide once sang—for it was then a fashionable centre and popular with the ducal court, whereas to-day it is a rather typical and not very exciting market town. What may turn the scales in its favour, indeed what will almost certainly do so, is the sight of Hoch-Osterwitz a little further up the valley, perched airily at a height of well over 2,000 feet on its isolated and precipitous limestone rock. It is a fine sight when the sun catches its walls and turns them almost white. The approach to the castle, which was rebuilt as a fortress against the Turks by Baron von Khevenhüller in 1570 but never put to the test of a siege, is partly hewn in the living rock and winds upwards, through fourteen successive gateways, to the keep in front of the castle. Therein you will find some interesting sixteenth-century armour. The church, with its 1720 high altar, should be visited too, and then, if you have a good head, you can return a different way, descending the abrupt Narren-Steig to the foot of the castle rock.

If time is short, however, it will be best to be content with a glimpse of St. Veit and of the Castle Osterwitz (equally picturesque on the left of the line when one comes by train from Bruck to Klagenfurt) from a distance, and to postpone visiting them to another time. We enter the Gurk valley near where the river Gurk turns abruptly south and where the narrow-gauge Gurktal railway begins its independent peregrinations. The line which runs up the valley alongside the country road looks as though it might be that of a toy railway, and I have seen a small child serenely playing in the middle of the permanent way while its mother worked in the field nearby. Evidently engine-drivers could be trusted to keep a good look-out.

The village of Gurk and its cathedral stand not at the head of the valley but half-way up where it has narrowed to a kind of waist with the woods sloping down to it on either side. The road winds through the valley beside the winding river, and presently we see rising in the very centre of the floor of the valley the two immense towers, topped in each case by the emblem of the sun, of Gurk cathedral, dominating completely the adjoining monastery which has belonged to the Redemptorists since 1923. One does not expect a church of this size and splendour in such a lonely rural spot. The towers had originally spires but when these were burnt they were replaced by the present sun-surmounted copper-green, onion-shaped, bulbous "growths". Gurk seems so far from the world and so far from any modern main route that it is hard to believe that Napoleon was here with his soldiers in 1808 and used the abbey buildings as a barracks.

The interior of the cathedral—romanesque and going back to a pillared basilica of yellowish limestone built between 1150 and 1220—contains a wealth of interest. Many generations have loved this great edifice and have spent their money to adorn it. The lower church, its vaulting supported by a hundred small white marble columns, was finished by 1174, when the bones of the Blessed Hemma of Friesach, the foundress and patron of the abbey, were transferred there. You can see her hat and her shoe —which anticipates the most recent fashion in shoes—beneath a glass case in the aisle. In the crypt you look down to the romanesque stone tomb, which has now been surmounted by a magnificent red marble altar with white reliefs: Italian work of 1720. The saint is depicted on her death-bed, while below, beneath the original sarcophagus, if we stoop to see it, is the romanesque head, a sort of primitive caryatid, which a sculptor cut to depict her nearly six centuries before. Extremely interesting too are the six painted wooden reliefs of episodes in the life of the saint and of her Crusader husband, which adorn the north and south walls of the transepts, the superb high altar (62) —where you should notice amongst a hundred other details of interest St. Luke with a cow kneeling beside him, the face of the evangelist being said to be the face of the carver himself. Rafael Donner's highly dramatic leaden Pietà, this sculptor's last work, is arresting also (61); but something of even greater interest awaits us when we mount the stairs at the west end of the church to visit the west gallery between the towers with its Bishop's

Chapel. The walls of this chapel are decorated with what has been described as "one of the most brilliant achievements of wall painting in Europe". No monochrome reproduction, alas, can give any idea of the lovely colouring, the pale egg-shell greens, of these early frescoes which depict Adam and Eve in Eden, the prophet Ezekiel and his two wheels, and other Biblical scenes. Gurk cathedral is not a building to be hurried through. Rather it is to be enjoyed step by step, noticing the elaborate canopy of its pulpit, noticing the stone inscribed with the name of the Celtic goddess of horses, Apona, which has been set in one of the columns, noticing the portrait of Thomas à Becket above an old altar stall, he having belonged to the same congregation as the monks originally here, noticing the frescoes on the north side of the west porch and noticing much else that is not only curious and interesting but also very lovely.

Returning to the main road from Gurk we can if we wish push on via Althofen to Friesach, once the most important Carinthian possession of the Archbishop of Salzburg, and to-day, with all its mediæval and Renaissance associations, one of the most beautiful small towns in Austria. Its lovely marble fountain came from the Renaissance palace of Tanzenberg nearby. A little south of the town the ruins of the church choir of what used to be the fortified deanery on the Virgilienberg (1309) suggest a stanza in Scott, by their lyrical and slightly melancholy charm. Further afield, situated at a height of over 4,000 feet and reached via Metnitz, is Flattnitz with its notable romanesque round church (52).

The drive to Gurk, through fields and orchards, past wooded hills; past—a typical feature—small wayside shrines with thatched or slatted roofs (46); past, perhaps, a great field of sunflowers which have been grown for their oil; past the white walls of farms on which are hanging the multitudinous bunches of ripening Indian corn; past the horizontal poles for drying hay which are known as *harpeen*; past the single vertical poles round which this and other crops are also wound for drying; past small white churches with curious roofs; past rounded green knolls topped by a farm building; past—for the fields are open—long, narrow stretches of rich clover or green sugar beet; past

52 FLATTNITZ: The church of a mountain village in Carinthia

53   MILLSTATT: The romanesque cloisters of the Monastery

54   MARIA SAAL: Contemporary carving of a Roman mailcart

ROMAN AND ROMANESQUE

everything which suggests the ordered life of the cultivator—all this will be so much indirect reward for the pilgrimage, whether pietistic or æsthetic, to the cathedral. The Austrian farmer owns his land: he is rarely, unless he rents parish land from his priest, a tenant. And Austria is a country for the most part of medium and small holdings, the medium with about sixteen acres of ploughland, the small with about two and a half.

What probably helps to preserve the integrity of Austrian farm life is that it is uncommercialised, it is still a community life. Agricultural wages are paid partly in kind, and may include wine, cider or apricot brandy. The doctor and the veterinary surgeon are sometimes paid in kind, and people like tailors and cobblers and seamstresses will come and stay on the farm while they do their work. Unmarried farmhands live with the family and sit at table with them, and the difference between employer and employee is only implied by certain subtle distinctions which are a matter of tact rather than hard-and-fast rule.

Costume, custom and rite all help to preserve the ancient modes of life. The people are proud of them. *Perchten* processions and bonfires at the time of the summer solstice go back, as Buschbeck points out, to pagan times, but the "star-singers" at Christmas, and the practice of writing the initials of the Three Wise Men on door lintels on Twelfth Night to guard the house during the ensuing year, are of Christian devisal. The same writer mentions the special customs relating to marriage, childbirth and death. Mirrors must be kept covered while the dead body is still in the house and the corpse must be carried out feet foremost "so that it cannot look back". When the cows descend from the "Alm" in autumn the leading cow not only carries a great bell but its horns are decorated with paper flowers and tinsel and a girl leads the procession distributing special pastry from a huge basket. The standing of drinks, as Buschbeck says, has the most strict traditions. "A young man would commit a *faux pas* in offering a glass of beer to one much older than himself. Generally speaking, treating, which is customary, is looked upon rather as a mark of esteem than as a mere means of increasing the intake of beer."

Not much further from Klagenfurt than Gurk but reached by a

considerably more roundabout route, because of the intervening Sau-Alpe, is Wolfsberg in the Levant valley, which has been called the "Paradise of Carinthia". The province has many lakes beside the Wörthersee, which was the one the composer Gustav Mahler preferred, coming many summers in succession and composing in a little hut above his woodland summerhouse at Maiernegg. The Millstättersee, the Ossiachersee, the Faakersee, or—over the border into East Tyrol but, like the Faakersee, most easily reached from Villach—the Weissensee (49), all have their adherents, and are all beautiful in their own way. In the middle of the Faakersee, which is quite a small lake, is an island and on the island a hotel where, if you cannot actually find nine bean rows and a hive for the honey bee to supply your modest wants, the excellent provender which is provided will go far to mitigate your disappointment. At Ossiach, on the Ossiachersee, you can sleep in what was formerly part of a Benedictine monastery and is now a hotel-pension, and when you have tired of bathing and crave altitude and solitude and a preliminary thrill, you have only to make your way to the west end of the lake and the Kanzel Aerial Railway—a mile and a half of cable with two supports en route—is there to take you and twenty-two other persons up almost to the top of the Kanzel (4,950 ft.), from which you can get a magnificent panorama of the countryside. There is a hotel on the terrace and in winter there is a ski lift to take skiers still higher. Since, despite all my efforts to overcome the disability in Switzerland, I still loathe being swung in mid-air, I have been content to let that small silver car soar heavenwards without me, cursing myself for a coward as I watched it go. I was ashamed of myself, and if any further sting to conscience were needed photographs of the view from the top provide it.

The Millstättersee is Carinthia's second largest lake. It is seven and a half miles long and is reached from Spittal (where you should certainly see the Italian-Renaissance courtyard of the Schloss) by post bus. The lake has exquisite surroundings and Millstatt itself is unspoilt, albeit highly popular with the discerning who pass their summers there. Not only the exquisite romanesque portal of the church which dates from about 1200 but the church itself and its arcaded cloisters are worthy of attention (53).

Spittal is reached from Villach, the "Town of Paracelsus", who lived there with his father for fourteen years. It has developed industrially, but, with the mountains looking down on it and with villages like Maria Gail within easy reach (40), it is worth visiting. The train takes one from Klagenfurt to Velden, to Villach, to Spittal and on, through the Tauern Tunnel, to Bad Gastein or by a side line to Lienz in East Tyrol. But one can make a far more dramatic exit from West Carinthia than this by road, since that world-famous piece of Alpine road engineering the Grossglockner Hochalpen Strasse was completed. It is—and justifiably—the best-known road in Europe and no one who traverses it is ever likely to forget it. Coming from Carinthia one ascends from Lienz via Mörtschach (55) to Heiligenblut, named from a phial of Holy Blood which the Blessed Briccius is said to have brought from Constantinople and which is preserved in the highly interesting parish church. In the severe winter of 1950–51 a terrible avalanche, an overflow from an immediately previous one on to what might have seemed a protective ledge or plateau above the village, swept down one night and killed twenty sleeping people, passing within a few yards of the school building, which remained untouched. From Heiligenblut onwards the constantly twisting and turning road becomes more and more dramatic until the Franz Josef Höhe above the Pasterzen glacier is reached, exactly facing the snow-covered flank of the Grossglockner. Here at a height of over 8,000 feet is a hotel worthy of Vienna which the enterprise of two local brothers from Dollach has, from earlier quite small beginnings, created. In summer it is nothing for them to serve over two thousand lunches in a day. In the hotel you will find not only the most modern cooking equipment but a portrait of the old Emperor after whom the spot is named. I have lunched out of doors on the terrace and basked in the sun as late as October 5th, although in another year the road might have been closed for the winter by then. One must descend from the Franz Josef Höhe a kilometre or two in order to recommence the ascent which will take one to the brief tunnel at the highest point of the road. There suddenly is revealed that panorama northwards of grey rock and scree which is the prelude to the even more dramatic and winding descent—skilfully negotiated by the long Alpine post cars—that, after what seems literally to have been the experience of careering over the mountain tops, will take one safely down to Bruck-Fusch near Zell-am-See.

55 The little village church of MÖRTSCHACH in the Mölltal

56 TRAUNKIRCHEN: The altar of the former Convent

57 MONDSEE: A Benedictine saint from an altar of the Collegiate Church (1681)

Meinrad Guggenbichler, sculptor

VII

Upper Austria

AGAIN and again I have seen faces light up at the mere
mention of the word Salzkammergut. It is not a musical
word. One might easily imagine that a German pedant was
getting excited about a new disease or that a zoologist was
warming up on the theme of some extremely rare species: "The
Salzkammergut, a distant relative of the marmot, unique in one
respect . . ." and so on. But to those who know their Austria the
Salzkammergut evokes not a hairy little animal but some of the
more peaceful and delightful scenery in the world. It calls up
visions of mirror-still, pale blue lakes, with tiny wooded head-
lands thrusting forth into them; of rocky pine-covered crags
descending sheer to the water; of gradually rising open green
slopes of pastureland and sunny orchard, dotted with farms and
backed by mountains and the dark forest.

For the Salzkammergut simply means "the district of the salt
mines" and it is a more or less happy accident that there should
be salt mountains when there is so much beautiful scenery or
such wealth and variety of landscape where there is so much salt.
Salt mines are not inimical to the landscape in the way that coal
mines are. You can borrow a costume rather like that of a pierrot
to wear over your own clothes and go down the salt mine at
Steinberg near Bad Aussee and toboggan on a bench on wheels,
rather like an elongated bobsleigh, for nearly a mile along rails
underground, before re-emerging, rather startled, into the
sunlight. Long before the Christian era the salt deposits at
Hellstadt had brought settlers to the place, who mined the salt
and carried it to the great highways to exchange for Roman
goods. Centuries later ingenious minds conceived the idea of
flooding the mine with water to dissolve the salt, and then
pumping the solution to saltpans which might be many kilometres distant and from which transport to the great cities would
be easier. Let no one imagine that salt will obtrude itself on his

attention in the way that it undoubtedly does when you visit the district around the Red Sea. The Salzkammergut is a green pleasance of perfect holiday country where, whoever else may be encountered, one will not come across Lot's Wife.

Though the greater part of it lies inside the province of Upper Austria its borders extend into both Styria and Salzburg. And indeed one is most likely to come to it either from Salzburg by the narrow-gauge railway which runs to St. Wolfgang and on to Bad Ischl, or else from Selzthal to Bad Aussee, which, as we have seen, is still in Styria. The Salzkammergut, which is enormously popular, is a district of lakes. Within a radius of twenty miles of Bad Ischl there must be—separated from one another by mountains or by lower hills—quite thirty lakes, several of them large, and one, the Attersee, the largest in Austria.

A lake as large as this—it is nineteen square miles—with banks which towards the north are flat, or merging into gently rolling country, will not make anyone feel claustrophobic. It is a very popular yachting centre; and, for those with a car, places as attractive as Steinbach and Weissenbach, or Seewalchem, at the other end of the lake, are an incentive to landcruise. The village of Attersee is popular with bathers and the lake steamer will take you to Weyregg nearby, where the mosaic pavement of a Roman villa has been discovered near the church. A little to the south of the lake rises the peak of the Schafberg, which dominates the Wolfgangsee and which to the north rises almost out of the waters of the Mondsee. The latter offers steamer excursions and bathing, and Mondsee itself, a pleasant market village closely linked with its rural area and with a church which is worth visiting (57). The little railway from Salzburg skirts the south-west bank of the Mondsee before turning due south to reach St. Eilgen, which lies at one end of the Wolfgangsee. All this is excellent walking country, and to the west lies the smaller Fuschl am See where there is an hotel in what was once the hunting lodge of the Archbishop of Salzburg and has since been the home of Ribbentrop.

One should come to St. Wolfgang not at the height of its season when there seems hardly room on the relatively small strip of land between the lakeside and the foot of the Schaffberg for the daily influx of charabancs, but after the season is over and the delightful village has, as it were, got its breath again. I remember leaving Bad Ischl late one afternoon in mid-October. The tiny train arrived from Goisern and out of it tumbled innumerable teen-aged schoolgirls, all in the charge of a single nun. Equally suddenly there sprang up from nowhere a horde of small schoolboys who were not concluding a hike as the girls were, but were waiting with their satchels to board the train and return to their homes. Certain carriages, however, had first to be shunted, and for five minutes I watched festoons of small boys push a truck, swing out of the sides of it, put coins on the rail to be flattened by its wheels and generally invite death at every instant. At last it was all done to the satisfaction of the solitary official, if not of the volunteer shunters, who seemed disappointed to be ordered on board. Off we set with much puffing of steam. But this was no ordinary train. It possessed a number of lovable eccentricities. Heading out of the town in one direction it rather quickly changed its mind, and, having nonchalantly crossed a river, started coming back in the diametrically opposite one. Actually this was reassuring, because I had felt sure from the start that the first direction was the wrong one. Seated in a second-class carriage half the size of a horse-box—through which the avalanche of amateur shunters had swept in an instant—I was presently visited by a rather rustic-looking ticket collector who had a monocle which he carefully screwed into his eye before inspecting my ticket. We plunged into a tunnel and the engine, always distinctly musical, began to play something exactly like the lovely *pas de deux* from the first act of *Giselle*. In addition to this accomplishment it had the loudest whistle I have ever heard on any engine, worthy of a transcontinental express. Halts were frequent and at every halt a group of happy children descended with their satchels. It was the daily homecoming. At last we reached a platform labelled St. Wolfgang. But it was not St. Wolfgang at all. Such a train would have scorned to do anything so pitifully obvious. St. Wolfgang was still the other side of the lake and in the dim evening light I and about a dozen schoolchildren transferred ourselves to the deck of a smart launch and crossed the still lake towards the lights ahead. I

151

stepped ashore a yard or two from the famous White Horse Inn, but all was silent, undisturbed and countrified, as unsophisticated as it should be, and the schoolchildren dispersed so quickly that in a moment I was left alone to make my way cautiously over the cobbles to the Hotel Post, where good food and a warm welcome awaited me.

This is the real St. Wolfgang, the St. Wolfgang that exists in the minds of its natives and that lingers in the memories of those visitors that have really loved the place. The little unhurried train had treated me well. A morning or two later, coming up from Salzburg, it put its brakes on and for some obstinate reason of their own they firmly refused to come off again. A brake is expected to be steadfast, but not quite as steadfast as this.

St. Wolfgang looks across its lake towards a pleasant green foreshore—the country through which the train runs—while behind it rise wooded slopes and a number of steeper variously shaped peaks. A lake like this and a view like this could keep anyone happy for months. A little way back from the village is the huge balk of the Schaffberg, which you can climb in three hours, or in two and a half hours if you wish to equal the record of the Duke of Windsor, who came here for some weeks soon after his abdication. If you do not feel like climbing, and it is still the season, a small cog-wheel railway will take you to the top of the mountain, from which you can get one of the finest views in Austria.

Although, apart from its hotels and a few shops, it is little more than a hamlet, St. Wolfgang is in possession of a great art treasure. Its patron saint is said to have built himself a chapel on the lakeside towards the end of the tenth century. The late-Gothic pilgrimage church was built between 1430 and 1470, and in 1471 a contract was signed with Master Michael Pacher of Bruneck for a high altar for the new church. He produced a masterpiece: it is the finest existent example of a German winged altar. Both the painting and the carving are the work of this Tyrolese artist, who, like many another great Austrian craftsman, combines a certain amount of Italian influence with native German feeling. The central group represents the coronation of the Virgin; the panels portray scenes from her life, including a rather realistic representation of the circumcision. Elsewhere in the church are a fine double altar by the baroque woodcarver Schwanthaler and by the north wall a somewhat distressing depiction of Christ crowned with thorns by Geggenbickler, who was also responsible for the pleasing baroque pulpit with its canopy on which lambs pasture amidst cherubs, overlooked by a figure of the Good Shepherd in a red robe and with a wide loose-rimmed black hat, who is carrying another lamb about his shoulders. The art of the woodcarver might almost be said to receive its apotheosis in the village church, where the faithful have been worshipping for nearly five centuries and to which art connoisseurs as well as pilgrims flock from all over the world.

Long before I knew Bad Ischl it was enthroned in my imagination as the spot so well loved by the Emperor Franz Josef and by his beautiful but temperamental consort. It is in the very centre of the Salzkammergut. Alas, each of us kills or helps to kill the thing he loves and it is doubtful whether its enjoyment of royal favour and resultant popularity with the fashionable world has added anything to its natural advantages beyond a Kurhaus and a number of hotels which already tend to date. It was here that in 1908 Edward VII showed his Daimler with such pride to the Emperor, who was not to be converted from his loyalty to the horse by it or any other self-propelled vehicle. If Bad Ischl has an air of faint loneliness to-day it is of loneliness for the parasol and the bustle. It has been a spa since 1822, and you can take brine baths or drink water from the Klebelsberg salt spring to the great benefit of the appropriate disorders. In fact the Hapsburgs were drawn to it in the first instance by the fact that an ancestor, the Archbishop-and-Duke Rudolph, had recovered his health there. Thither, too, in the autumn of 1853 had come to the Kaiser Villa, which at that time was only rented by the Imperial family from a rich burgher, the young Emperor, to meet his cousins "Neni" and "Sisi" who with their mother were installed in an hotel in the town square. The two fond mothers—who were sisters—had planned a match between Neni and her cousin, but it was the sixteen-year-old Sisi whom he instantly preferred and to whom he made his declaration. Some years later the Arch-duchess Sophie bought the Kaiser Villa for the young couple. It is a modest enough country house standing in parkland just on the outskirts of the town and you can visit it and see it very much as it was in the days of its royal occupation, family photographs and all. It is full of gifts and purchases and hunting souvenirs, bearing the most eloquent testimony to the acquisitiveness of a period and its execrable taste, as well as to its capacity for the destruction of wild life. My admiration for that stern slave of duty and, in many ways, that lovable old man Franz Josef was put to a severe test as I wandered through these rooms. Hung on the walls, suitably mounted on a board and embellished with date and venue, are the frontals and horns of, I think, every chamois he ever shot. There were 2,036 in all, and the 2,000th one was particularly lucky, as it got stuffed and can be seen now intact, a graceful creature, and not even moth-eaten. Here, hard by the travelling sedan of his mother, the Archduchess Sophie, are the horns of the first, accounted for—oh, thrilling moment in the life of youth—in the year 1849. And here is the last, shot at Helmesriesen, September 4th, 1911, when he was eighty-one. (The last deer would be at Rammgraben, August 23rd, two years later.) There is a white chamois accounted for in Ischl, a boar that weighed 480 lb. from Hungary, a bear from Russia in 1874. In sixty-five years of shooting, the carefully kept records of his shooting books show that he had dispatched 50,556 head of game. I confess that these figures fill me with a certain awe, that one human being should wreak so much destruction on the creatures of the field and forest and snows.

But if the ghost of the white chamois ever returns to haunt these rooms where its frontal still hangs, it perhaps pauses reflectively in front of a leather-topped writing table which, innocent though it looks, is the symbol of a far greater destruction wrought by man, not on his creature kindred but on his kind. For at this table in July 1914 the Emperor signed his ultimatum to Serbia. We need not be too severe on him.* They had deliberately delayed giving the old man the well-reasoned

* It was the folly of certain ministers and high Army officials and not any belligerency in the monarch himself that for months previously and even years had longed for an opportunity to humiliate Serbia.

protests of his Hungarian minister Tisza, warning him that the war for which his General Staff were pressing would prove fatal to Austria. As he signed the document at this table, decorated with snapshots of his grandchildren, this octogenarian, whose white china ewer and white basin sunk in its plain enamel washstand you can see in the adjoining bedroom, eloquent testimony to the simplicity of the Imperial tastes, could hardly have been expected to know that he was signing the death warrant not only of his own but of half a dozen other European dynasties.

In the town on the river front is the Franz Lehar villa which is also open to visitors and where you can study the taste of the composer of *The Merry Widow* in his many purchases. It is quite execrable, and as the words fall on your ears, "This is a Rembrandt" (!), "This is a Vandyke" (! !), "This sideboard is a present from Daly's Theatre in 1912", "This is the late Franz Lehar's champagne cooler. Alas, it seems to be empty", "This is—a naughty girl" (nude Circe in ivory, beside a silver boar!), and as you pass from one monstrous inscribed photograph to the next (wide grins, small hats, hobble skirts, the most hideous women's fashions ever seen) and from one sentimental nude of the early 1900's to its very similar neighbour, you are almost put in the mood to thank God for Picasso. At last, in the room in which Lehar died, which has been left exactly as it was then, with even the medicine bottles beside the table, you find a different note; the taste here is more personal, the treasures are baroque, catholic and possessed of dignity, and you feel relieved that the composer should have chosen to die out of sight of all his other dreadful bric-à-brac.

Bad Ischl is built on a sandwich of land between the river Ischl and the river Traun, just before they merge. The former has come from the Wolfgangsee; and you can follow the latter upstream to the Hallstattersee or downstream to the Traunsee, Austria's deepest lake, which the Romans called "felix", the happy one. The Traunsee is well worth visiting, not only for its own sake but if it were only to see the lake castle of Orth as it were floating on the lake on its tiny islet (58) or to visit down the lake on its western side. Facing the Traunstein across the water, this village with its delightful small rocky promontory projecting into the lake, tree-covered and crowned by the old Johannes-Kirche, is an idyllic spot. Happy indeed anyone who has the time to linger there. Altmünster is further down the lake on the same bank. Gmunden at the north end of the lake is a much larger place than either of these, with a leafy esplanade. Ebensee, at the opposite end of the lake, where the river enters it, has salt works which were originally constructed in 1607.

From Bad Ischl the road follows the river the whole way via Goisern to Hallstatt in its almost unique situation on the south-west bank of the lake of that name. Tucked under the mountain-side, indeed one might almost say partially clinging to it, and with the foundations of some of its houses actually in the lake, Hallstatt basks in the morning sun but loses it fairly early in the afternoon because of the salt mountain which rises immediately behind it. It is a fascinating village, with a history that goes back to the fourteenth century. The very fact that by the nature of its site it must be cribbed, cabined and confined adds to its attractions. The bus stops a tactful few hundred yards short of where the village street begins. For reasons of space, the picturesque Corpus Christi "procession" is held on the lake in boats because there is more room there. The same custom prevails at Traun-kirchen. If you are buried in Hallstatt you are only allowed to remain ten years in your grave. After that—again for reasons of space—your bones and your skull are exhumed and go to join thousands of other skulls, some of them going back to the fifteenth century, which lie with their names painted on them in the charnel-house.

Above Hallstatt and on the way to its salt mine is the site of the very early burial ground which was discovered in 1846 and which has given its name, the Hallstatt Period, to the time—tenth to fifth century B.C.—when it was in use. We can cross the lake by boat and take the train—the same which comes from Selzthal in Styria to Bad Ischl—or go by road, up the valley to Obertraun, which is the starting point for the long but rewarding expedition to the famous Dachstein ice caves, which are well lit but which must be visited with a guide. The ascent of the Dachstein itself is a sterner undertaking and is for experts only.

I have already alluded briefly to Bad Aussee in an earlier

58 SCHLOSS ORTH on its island in the Traunsee

59   The Stiftshof Courtyard (1626–70)

60   The Bruckentor Gate (1667–1745)
Jakob Prandauer, architect

THE MONASTERY OF KREMSMÜNSTER

chapter. We are still in the Salzkammergut but we are back by now in the province of Styria. Bad Aussee, in the high mountain valley of the Traun, is a pleasant spot for visitors either in summer or in winter. We may stand in no need of its brine baths and we may have no wish to indulge in winter sports. Even so I believe this market village is bound to endear itself to us. The woods rise around it so gently, the air is so clear and sweet, the school-children look healthy and happy, the very fields, pines and larches seem to take us to their hearts. Three miles away is Alt Aussee on the edge of its lake, which offers excellent bathing. And about the same distance, but to the east of Bad Aussee, is Grundlesee, a lake favoured by fishermen and an ideal place for a holiday far from crowds. You can climb from there up to the Toplitzsee, with its very steep wooded sides, and to the tiny sheltered Kammersee, enjoying a visit to the two waterfalls at the same time.

Alt Aussee can boast, if that is the right word, of having had in its possession at one time what was the largest and most valuable horde of looted works of art in the history of the world. The Nazis made its salt mountain the depository of pillage from all over occupied Europe. Following the example of the French under Napoleon—who, however, forbore trying to *destroy* their acquisitions when defeated—the Germans helped themselves to what they liked. Much of it was hidden in the salt mine at Alt Aussee, and when defeat seemed near, bombs were placed in each cavern of the Steinberg mine which might have destroyed the Van Eyck altar-piece from Ghent, Michelangelo's "Madonna and Child", the Czernin Vermeer, Titians, Breughels, multiple thefts from Naples Museum and countless other treasures. The bombs were secretly removed by the local miners, who had their own means of access to them, and who were more concerned that their salt mountain should not collapse under the explosion and rob them of their means of livelihood, than that one of the loveliest Vermeers in existence should perish.

I have said nothing as yet of the capital of Lower Austria. Linz, if we would see it in its most favourable aspect, should be approached by river. The river Danube takes somewhat a bend as it enters and leaves the town—not equal, however, to that incredible bend in open country near Schlögen where it doubles on its own track, making a loop rather like a thrown lasso. Linz occupies both banks, though chiefly the right one. Linz is the third largest town in Austria and has a history which links it back with the Roman Lentia and, later, with the Babenbergs. At first it supported the Reformation, and Johannes Kepler taught mathematics here at the Protestant provincial school from 1612 to 1626 and wrote his first work while pursuing those duties. It was the *Harmony of the World*. A planetary and mathematical harmony chiefly, even then, rather than a human one, for in the very year the treatise was completed the peasants' war brought besiegers—unsuccessfully—to the walls of the city. Later the Counter-Reformation made itself vigorously felt in Linz. Linz has a good museum, where you will locate some of the Hallstatt finds, and its environs are pleasant, notably the Pöstlingberg, which can be reached by tram and from which one gets an excellent view back over the city as well as of more distant reaches of the Danube as it crosses the plain. Linz, by the way, was the possessor of the first "railway" line ever constructed in Europe, a horse railway, not a steam railway, along which, about the time of Schubert, rail carriages used to be drawn, with passengers on their way to the country and to Bohemia.

For many, the most cogent reason for a visit to Linz will be that it lies within easy reach of the three great abbeys, the Cistercian abbey of Wilhering, the Benedictine abbey of Kremsmünster and the even more famous Augustinian abbey of St. Florian.

An enthusiast may enlighten us more than a dozen dispensers of guarded judgments and therefore I will quote forthwith a little of Sacheverell Sitwell's praises of Wilhering. He writes in his introduction to *German Baroque Sculpture*: "It is essential to call attention to Wilhering. . . . For Wilhering represents the best rococo in Austria. There is nothing whatever in the overrated Salzburg that is upon this level. Wilhering belongs to that apogee of the rococo which is nearly indescribable in words. Its shimmering, flickering colours and the incredible grace of its door frames and picture frames are no subjects for dull prose. But they possess an unerring grace which it would have seemed impossible

to express within the limits of Christian architecture, even
when its accompaniment may have been the anthems or masses
of Haydn. There is nothing in Austria comparable with Wilhering. . . ." My immediate impulse is to counter this with:
"There is nothing in Austria comparable with the interior which
Prandtauer planned for St. Pölten." But we are not running off
the Baroque Plate or the Rococo Stakes, and the enthusiasm of
one individual offers no direct threat to that of another. The
architect of Wilhering abbey church remains unidentified. Sitwell attributes it to Andreas Altomonte, member of a family
originally from Genoa, and a relative of Bartolomeo Altomonte
who painted the frescoes and Martino Altomonte who painted
the altar panels for the church. Despite its exuberance the pulpit
is a magnificent piece of work. If one can speak in relation to
human beauty, of

> That infinitesimal more which itself is all
> 'Twixt beauty and beauty missed, to delight our sight.

one is always, or nearly always, conscious, in relation to rococo,
of that infinitesimal more which may be, or which might so
easily have been, just too much. But neither at Wilhering nor at
St. Pölten is this thought present to our minds. There is an
abundance, but it is an abundance of which we feel disposed to
shed practically nothing. After the fire in 1733 (one sometimes
wonders whether abbots of this period welcomed fires as an
excuse for rebuilding) only the church and part of the newly-
planned buildings for the monastery were completed. In the
picture gallery will be found works by both the Altomontes,
Schmidt Kremser and Maulpertsch.

Kremsmünster is interesting quite as much for the monastery
buildings (59, 60) as for the monastery church. It is the oldest
remaining abbey in Upper Austria and was founded by that rival
of Charlemagne, Duke Tassilo of Bavaria, in 777, who, with two
other giant statues, can be seen over the entrance arch against a
background of white shells. The baroque at Kremsmünster has
been described as a cross-section over one and a half centuries of
art evolution. Zürn's marble angels on the altars of the abbey
church are charged with an emotion not dissimilar to that which

inspired Ublherr's stucco figure of St. Elizabeth on the high altar
at Wilhering perhaps as much as half a century later. In each case
the figures parade their intention not reticently but unashamedly.
They are meant to stir us. The tradition is established and knows
exactly what it wants to achieve. As Pevsner points out, the
methods of the *stuccatori* right up to the middle of the eighteenth
century were still mediæval. They thought of themselves as
craftsmen embarked upon a joint adventure rather than in terms
of individual vindication. If talent was there it voiced itself, but
it did so without personal idiosyncrasy. If it was not there, then
pious intention revealed, as it was bound to do, its own in-
sufficiency. Perhaps this is why a baroque masterpiece always
seems like a happy accident. Perhaps it is one; the spontaneous
overflow of genius out of the cup of consecrated craftsmanship.

Some years after the first world war and before ever the
second world war was yet clearly visible upon the horizon the
monks at Kremsmünster were forced to sell their greatest art
treasure, the Reydams tapestries, to the Metropolitan Museum
in New York. For the plain truth is that monasteries such as this,
and all the great monasteries in Upper and Lower Austria, pre-
suppose a Church which was not only wealthy but part of the
very fabric of the Empire. You have only to look at the Kaiser
Saal here, or at Melk, or at St. Florian to get an idea with what
splendour the princes of the Church saw fit to entertain the
princes of the State. The Holy Roman Emperor might be an
honoured guest at a monastery and must have somewhere where
he could give audience. The Kaiser Saal at Kremsmünster is
decorated with stuccoes by Diego Francesco Carlone, who was
probably responsible for the charming rococo figures of Veritas
and Virtus in the Stucco Gallery of the Ludwigsburg Palace near
Stuttgart, and who is also represented by work at St. Florian and
Einsiedeln. In the Kremsmünster Kaiser Saal is a great white and
gold tiled stove which is quite as fine as, if not possibly finer than,
anything to be seen at Schönbrunn or in the Hofburg. The
monastery has two strange features, an eight-storey building not
unlike a prophecy in baroque of the future skyscraper; and—
more famous still—its five-arcaded fish preserves, decorated with
fountain statues and each with its separate lock and key, where

61 Pietà (1740–41)
Raphael Donner, sculptor

62 A bishop on the baroque
High Altar

Michael Hönel, sculptor

GURK CATHEDRAL

63   ST. FLORIAN: The main portal (1713) to the Monastery
Jakob Prandtauer, architect ; Leonard Sattler, sculptor

the fish are said to have been summoned successfully to their meals by the ringing of a bell.

Liberalism, which promised us the moon—not yet safely delivered—and which has, unquestionably, ameliorated the lot of many of the more wretched, has, at the same time, disrupted life by contributing, intentionally or unintentionally, to the over-throw of an outlook so confident of the future that men were content to spend half a century or more on the completion of a building which was to glorify God down the centuries. Humanity plants trees, builds houses, cultivates land and founds a family with most satisfaction when it looks back on an intelligible past and foresees an attainable future. Religion which presupposes continuity, a continuity of interest on the part of heaven in the affairs of earth, furnishes something for which theories and political slogans and quiet returns are no effective substitute. The baroque building period, which recreated the Abbey of St. Florian (63), lasted from 1686 until 1751. Architects, builders, painters, sculptors, stucco workers and craftsmen all contributed their share and were content to labour for a distant future. Three architects were jointly responsible: Carlo Antonio Carlone (d. 1708), who began the work and planned the abbey church; Jacob Prandtauer (1660–1726), whom we have to thank for the summer refectory, the magnificent staircase tract, the marble hall, etc.; and Gotthart Heyberger, who completed the library. The open staircase hall at St. Florian, with its white façade, its series of two-storeyed arcaded openings either side of the central archway into the courtyard, and its lovely wrought-iron gates on each landing of the stairway, is one of Prandtauer's happiest inspirations, gracious to a degree, yet without ostenta-tion. In the monastery are a whole series of apartments splendidly furnished for the Holy Roman Emperor should he come, frescoes of hunting scenes and a gilded and rococo bed which Sitwell ascribes without hesitation to a member of the Carlone family. It is all on a note of magnificence, just as the church with its elaborate choir stalls and its lofty choir organ strikes a similar note, a church not as ethereally gracious as Arlesheim or as gravely moving as Einsiedeln, but imposing and with some beautiful white stuccoes by Bartolommeo Carlone.

When at St. Florian the musical should recall for a moment the figure of that so-called "rival" of Brahms—rival in the sense that like Wolf he was in the opposite Wagner camp—Anton Bruckner. Vienna is proud of Bruckner, but it is the province of Upper Austria which can count him truly her own. Born in 1824 as son to the village schoolmaster in Ausfelden, Bruckner's earliest musical loyalty was to the organ, a loyalty never revoked. At thirteen he became a choirboy at St. Florian, and to St. Florian after many vicissitudes in a small village school he returned as a teacher in 1845. Twenty-three years would pass before he would be called to Vienna as a Professor in the Conservatorium. Wagner converted Bruckner from classicism to romanticism, a conversion already detectable on the horizon in the D Minor Mass composed at St. Florian in 1864. At the monastery you can see his grand piano brought here from Vienna and the bed in which he died. The modest Bruckner, deeply distressed by the wickedness of man, but with an unquenchable faith in God to counter his melancholy, is a lovable figure, and when success eventually comes his way and Vienna University honours him, while the Emperor gives him a room in the Belvedere, we feel, just as we feel in the case of Haydn, that virtue has been vindicated and that the fairy tale has had a happy ending as all fairy tales should.

VIII

Salzburg

SALZBURG should beware lest it succumb to the deadly sin of vanity. It stands in mortal danger. People flock to it from all over the world. The most famous conductors are proud to give their services at its festival. Music lovers who find themselves sleeping in a bath there in July or August count themselves fortunate, even if the tap drips. And now Nature has seen fit to pay the city one more and most delicate compliment. The sea-gulls have discovered it. In winter they come all the way from East Prussia, spend the day on the river being fed by the in habitants, and depart to Chiemsee in Bavaria for the night. Let the hoteliers of Salzburg take note of this last fact and let it curb their elation. It is significant that even the seagulls feel that Salzburg is difficult when it comes to sleeping-quarters.

Places pay the penalty for their popularity. Or do they make us pay for it? The dearest cup of tea ever lifted to my lips was brought to me on the restaurant terrace on top of the Mönchs-berg. Perhaps if bills preceded rather than succeeded our light refreshments I might have had the presence of mind to imitate that superb gesture of King David (when his three comrades-in-arms brought him the cup of water from the well at Bethlehem for which they might have had to pay with their lives) by pouring my tea out on the ground and explaining to the astonished waitress that I felt it would have been unseemly for me to swallow anything quite so costly. The opportunity may occur again. But can I be sure that the restaurant proprietor will know his Bible well enough for the thrust to go home?

To those who love Salzburg, and they are legion, all this will seem in very poor taste. When I first met Stefan Zweig he was already an exile from his beloved Austria, but the memory of his Salzburg home glowed in his heart in a way that nothing else did. He would never see it again, but I have only to turn to his autobiography to know how he felt about it: "Of all Austrian towns Salzburg seemed to me the most ideal . . . it was then not yet the meeting place for the 'prominent' of the earth or famous for its festival plays, but an old-time, sleepy, romantic little town on that last slope of the Alps where the hills gently resigned themselves to the German plain. The little wooded hill on which I lived was the dying wave, so to speak, of the mighty mountain chain; inaccessible to automobiles and attainable only by a hundred or more stairs up a way of the cross that was over three centuries old, the effort was rewarded by an enchanting view over the roofs and gables of the many-steepled city." I have climbed the many steps to that house myself, which is in other possession now. It is a long house, one room deep, flattened up against a fortress wall upon the Kapuzinerberg, not much more than ten minutes' walk from the centre of the town. When Zweig took possession of it immediately after the first world war, conditions in the city were grim: "We found our home in almost uninhabitable condition. The rain dripped merrily into the rooms, after every snowfall the halls were flooded. A thorough repair of the roof was impossible because the carpenters had no timber for rafters, the tinsmith no lead for gutters; the worst leaks were painstakingly covered with tar paper and when fresh snow fell there was no alternative to a personal clambering on the roof so as to remove the load in good time." But better times were to come. He could write of only a few years later: "A remarkable thing had come about quite silently. The little town of Salzburg with its forty thousand inhabitants, which I had selected for its romantic remoteness, had become amazingly transformed: it had become the summer artistic capital, not only of Europe but of the whole world. Max Reinhardt and Hugo von Hofmannsthal, in order to alleviate the plight of actors and musicians who were unemployed during the summer months of the hard post-war years, had arranged a few performances, notably that famous outdoor production of *Everyman* on the Domplatz. . . . Little by little the world began to take notice. The best conductors, singers, actors, competed ambitiously for the opportunity to disclose their talents. . . . These extraordinary performances became something that none wanted to miss. Kings and princes, American millionaires and

film-stars, music lovers, artists, poets and snobs would assemble
in Salzburg. . . . In summer one encountered on its streets everybody from America and Europe who sought the highest
manifestations of art, in Salzburg costumes; white linen shorts
and jackets for the men, the gay *dirndls* for the women. Diminu-
tive Salzburg suddenly set the world's fashions. . . . Thus I
found myself in my own town in the centre of Europe. Fate had
granted a wish of mine which I had hardly dared dream, and our
house on the Kapuzinerberg had become a European house. . . .
Romain Rolland stayed with us and Thomas Mann; among
writers, H. G. Wells, Hofmannsthal, Jakob Wassermann, Van
Loon, James Joyce, Emil Ludwig, Franz Werfel, Georg Brandes,
Paul Valéry, Jane Addams, Scholem Asch, Arthur Schnitzler
were welcome guests; among musicians, Ravel and Richard
Strauss, Alban Berg, Bruno Walter, Bartok, and many others
among painters, actors, scientists, and scholars from the four
corners of the world. . . . One day Arturo Toscanini climbed
the steep way to us and in that hour a friendship began which
enabled me to love and enjoy music even more and more under-
standingly than before. For years thereafter I was a faithful
attendant at his rehearsals. . . .''

One could scarcely have a better summary of what the 1920's
did for Salzburg. Here is in epitome the city's recent history. It
shot into favour. Its population is now three times that which
Zweig mentions, an increase not wholly favoured by the native
and partly fostered by the fact that after the second world war it
became a centre for the disposition of displaced persons, many
of whom have remained. The festival has brought money to the
owners of hotels and pensions for many miles round, a fact they
are inclined to forget when it comes to helping to cover the
almost inevitable deficit on an undertaking of the kind. It is
genuinely cultural and international in conception and its
musical importance, in the eyes of those who run it, completely
outweighs all commercial implications. Salzburg is a great
musical centre. One should remember that even when drinking
tea on the Mönchsberg.

The Mönchsberg and the Kapuzinerberg are relatively small
eminences out in the plain, and separated from one another, as

though split apart, by the passage of the river Salzach. Salzburg clusters in the gap between, and the older part of the town, where most of the buildings of importance are to be found, lies on the left bank where there is more room, and under the Mönchsberg which is crowned by the great fortress Hohensalzburg, founded in 1077 by Archbishop Gebhard, but owing most of its salient features to reconstruction about 1500 by Archbishop Leonhard. Salzburg has a long Christian history, and one which is almost unique in certain ways. There are catacombs right in the face of the Mönchsberg, at the back of St. Peter's Abbey, which possibly date from the early third century, and this may have been the first place of Christian worship on Austrian soil. We hear vaguely of a St. Maximus at this time, about whom, however, very little is known. In 477 the Roman town—which was called Juvavum—was destroyed, and history remains silent until about 700 A.D., when Theodor, Duke of Bavaria, bestowed the site of Juvavum, as well as the salt mines at Reichenhall, upon St. Hruodpert (Rupert), who came from Franconia to found the Benedictine Monastery of St. Peter and the Convent on the Nonnberg. Abbots, bishops, archbishops, these are the people to whom Salzburg henceforward will owe its history. It is a history of the building of churches, the acquisition of territory, the foundation of great monasteries. The *Book of Austria* can speak of Leonhard von Keutschach as "the first of that line of sharp-profiled religious princes, concerning whom there has been much conflict of opinion, who during the changing periods of gothic, renaissance and baroque styles, placed on the face of Salzburg the stamp and sign of their own self-willed and often secular personalities." But was he the first? By despatching the town councillors in chains to Radstadt because they claimed the right to take orders from the Emperor rather than from him Keutschach made clear the pretensions of the archdiocese. But Salzburg had had the right (granted to it by the Emperor Charles IV) to make gold coins since 1366 and silver since 996, and from the moment when Conrad I (d. 1147) left St. Peter's Monastery for a residence of his own in the town the conception of bishop-rule may be said to have been clearly visible on the horizon.

Taine took the Roman papal state of his day as the text for a fierce attack on the secular arm of the papacy. I can imagine a rabid Protestant to-day using the stones of Salzburg—which has been called the German Rome—to point the moral against the concentration of too much worldly power in the hands of clerics. I have not so much in mind that Salzburg is a city of churches. There were twenty-eight of them in Mozart's time, for a population of twenty thousand, and when the cathedral was built to hold ten thousand, the entire population of the city was then only eight thousand. Its rulers saw Salzburg as a great Christian centre, a meeting-place for the faithful from all parts of the Germanic empire, so that the number of churches had no direct relationship to the number of citizens. But with the election by the prelates of the cathedral in 1587 of the amazing Wolf Dietrich von Raitenau to be—at the age of twenty-eight—Prince and Archbishop of Salzburg a phase of magnificence begins which, whether we see it as a late flowering of the Renaissance or as part of that triumphant expression of relief at the success of the Counter-Reformation—and in fact it was a little of each—would blossom into some strange extravagances not too easily reconcilable with the spirit, say, of St. Francis.

The "religiously-worldly archbishop", as he has been called with some venom, spent, after twenty-four years of government, the last eight years of his life in the Hohensalzburg as the prisoner of his successor, Marcus Sitticus. But before this incarceration he had had time to inaugurate the building of the new cathedral, having pulled down what remained, after a fire, of the old romanesque cathedral (some people say that he had it set on fire). He had been responsible for the Residenz, the Chapter House, the Royal Stables, the Cloister Walk, the Gabriels-Kapelle (his mausoleum) in the cemetery of St. Sebastian, the pleasure palace of Altenau (built by him in 1606 for Salome Alt and renamed Schloss Mirabell by Marcus Sitticus), the Neugebäude with tower (now the belfry for the Glockenspiel), the shambles on the river (18 Gries Gasse), and the Augustine Monastery, and had enlarged the Franciscan Monastery—not too bad a record for one individual, even when he is in a position to sign himself "Archiepiscopus et Princeps", as Dietrich and all his successors would now do. What had been a mediæval see

171

became the court of a prince. Salzburg began its great musical tradition. The Salzburger Hofkapelle was founded in 1591 and both German and Italian composers contributed music for the new cathedral, in which the Cathedral Dedication Mass of Orazio Belevoli, employing three organs and eight different choirs on twelve different balconies, would be sung in 1628. Nor was secular music forgotten. Eleven years before this, Sitticus had had an open-air theatre cut out of the rocks at Hellbrunn. In this theatre an opera called *Andromeda* and Monteverdi's *Il Orfeo* would be the first two operas ever performed north of the Alps. Before long the Archbishop would have his own baroque stage in the Italian style in his town residence.

Marcus Sitticus had strengthened the fortifications. His successor, Paris Lodron, successfully kept Salzburg out of the Thirty Years War. Kuenburg, Thun (who made use of the services of Fischer von Erlach and who augmented his finances by income from mines and from the Dutch East India Company) and Firmian (who gave Goethe a theme for *Hermann und Dorothea* by banishing 30,000 Protestants from the province in a single year) carried on the tradition of this episcopal principality, which continued to enjoy its independence until Napoleon secularised it in 1803, when it became an electorate and the Grand Duke Ferdinand of Tuscany its first elector. In 1805 the Emperor of Austria assumed sovereignty over it by the Treaty of Pressburg. In 1809 the French were administering it and in 1810 by the Treaty of Vienna it became a Bavarian province. In 1816 it was returned to Austria minus the Berchtesgaden district. Its political vicissitudes were for the moment over.

We should see the city and its buildings against this historical background. Although Hellbrunn and the Mirabell are fantastic enough—especially when we come to visit their gardens—the baroque of many of the Salzburg churches is definitely restrained. Indeed, if we want to get a new and rather different impression of baroque we will begin by visiting the Kollegienkirche (64). Fischer's plan for the University Church, combining the long nave and central dome and transepts, it has been said, reflects the study of Vignola and perhaps the church of St. Andrea in Mantua, which was the work of Alberti. The whole lofty interior of the

64 SALZBURG: The dome of the University Church
(Kollegienkirche) (1694-1707)

Fischer von Erlach, architect

173

65 SALZBURG PANORAMA: The Kollegienkirche is in the foreground, behind it are the twin towers of the Cathedral, and looking down on the town is the Castle

church with the great circle of the cupola, the high vaulted aisles, the apse with its stucco decoration, the fine organ gallery, the sixteen archways in the walls, the eight marble balconies are neo-classical almost in their extreme simplicity and restfulness. Is this a happy accident because no later hands have essayed embellishment, so that there is the same and indeed an even greater feeling of space than there is in the cathedral? The whole conception is restrained and yet gracious. The side chapels are hidden from view, reached by archways over which a most beautiful oval frame in stucco, decorated with flowers, leads the eye up to a balcony through which the interior of the chapel is once more visible. And between these two side chapels we see the apse, held together by two huge pillars without tectonic function, a breakwater, as it were, between the nave and that huge wave of stucco decoration which foams up from behind the altar, half concealing one window, around the higher oval one. It is hard to give any idea of the lightness and grace of this choir of angels floating about the serene figure of the Immaculata. The effect is of light, floating, fleecy clouds everywhere; the figures emerge from the clouds, or the clouds boil up around them. It is not difficult to believe that this lovely work came mainly from the same hand, that of Diego Francisco Carlone, which was responsible for the exquisite grace of Veritas and Virtus at the Ludwigsburg Palace near Stuttgart. Carlone, though he may have owed much to his Italian origin, lived and worked north of the Alps from the start of his career until he was almost seventy, and his work suggests that Germany of the eighteenth century to which not only the art of the *stuccatori* but that of the porcelain-maker owes so much.

The University Church faces north-east across the square where Salzburg's vegetable market is held. Its façade is striking (64). The nave projects itself forward between flanking prismatic towers, the middle axis extending upwards to reach its culmination in the statue of the Madonna, while behind, dominating the whole conception, rises the mighty cupola. The façade of Fischer's next undertaking, Holy Trinity Church, shows the emergence of a more personal style. Its wider site had encouraged the architect to attempt something almost as dramatic in its way as the Karlskirche in Vienna. No one who has seen Holy Trinity floodlit by night is likely to forget it. The façade is convex, as against the concave of the earlier Kollegienkirche. The interior of the church is equally spacious, equally restrained. In his third and smaller creation, the St. Johannesspitalskirche, we find the same planned adjacency to certain related buildings, an exterior that is somewhat cubic in appearance, the receding layers being superimposed upon one another, not like the rear of the Kollegienkirche; and an interior equally simple and made equally gracious by the judicious use of stucco decoration. There is both daring and an exquisite sense of symmetry in the arrangement of the four windows—one sickle-shaped, another, high above it, oval—behind and either side of the altar. The decorative work is never excessive and always appropriate, and when we stand back and view it as a whole we are given the measure of the mind that planned and the hand that executed.

The Cathedral is late Renaissance and early baroque and under its high altar rest the relics of the first Bishop of Salzburg, St. Rupert. It was not he, however, but St. Virgil who built a romanesque basilica on this site in 767. Pictures of Salzburg in the fifteenth and sixteenth centuries show a huge five-towered basilica in the form of a cross, of which hardly a relic remains. Wolf Dietrich made what must have been almost a clean sweep of the centre of the city in 1598. The plans for the new cathedral which Vincenzio Scamozzi drew up for him were too grandiose even for Dietrich to contemplate and others for a simpler and slightly smaller building were substituted. Actually it was his successor, Marcus Sitticus, who laid the foundation stone in 1614, and it was the architect Santino Solari who was responsible for what has been called the purest Italian structure north of the Alps. The cupola, the twin towers and in fact the whole of the white and rose Untersberg marble façade are typical baroque and in keeping with the other churches in the town. Crowning the centre of the façade, between the two towers, is the statue of Our Lord, a wonderful sight against the Salzburg blue sky. Beneath are the coats-of-arms of Marcus Sitticus and Paris Lodron, flanked by statues of Moses and Elias, while other statues, of St. Rupert, St. Virgil, St. Peter and St. Paul, flank the three windows immediately below. The interior of the cathedral is simple and the few decorations are early baroque. The famous Resurrection on the high altar is by Mascagni.

With the building of the new cathedral the Franziskanner-kirche, which is only a few hundred yards away, ceased to possess parochial rights, becoming, in 1635, solely the church of the monastery. It lies beyond the Domplatz, in the centre of which is Hagenauer's statue of Our Lady of the Immaculate Conception, a beautiful piece of work, although many have thought it markedly secular and indeed almost sensuous in feeling. Below the statue itself are the figures of an Angel, Wisdom, the Devil and the Church, cast in lead. With its dark thirteenth-century romanesque nave, its romanesque south portal, its lofty and well-lit choir with reticulated vaulting, the Franzis-kannerkirche, or Franciscan Church, is a combination of the three main European styles, Romanesque, Gothic and Baroque. The high altar which Michael Pacher, the famous Tyrolese wood-carver and painter of the late Gothic period, carved for the church and on which he worked until his death in 1498 survives only in its central figure, a most lovely Madonna which adorns the present baroque altar. The figure of the child has been added.

If the Franziskannerkirche has had a number of changes made in it, this is nothing to the many metamorphoses through which St. Peter's Abbey Church (66) has passed. The original church founded by St. Rupert stood a little further south against the rock at the foot of the Mönchsberg to which doubtless it gave a name. The foundations of the tower of the present church belong to the Carolingian epoch (847) and the basic structure itself dates from 1130, the earlier building having been destroyed by fire. Starting from its basic conception—a basilica with a projecting transept above a crypt, three apses, a flat-roofed nave and cross groin vaulted side aisles—we find successive abbots transforming it, adding to it, and subtracting from it, raising the tower, more than once, raising the height of the nave, abolishing the side-apses, and in 1756—the year of the birth of Mozart—giving it its beautifully balanced dome. We get an epitome of its many transmutations in its romanesque portal, within the tower porch, which has sculptures of about 1240 and a door with rich rocaille work which dates from 1766. In the church you can see amongst other interesting things such as the wrought-iron screens, the tomb of Michael Haydn, brother of the composer; a memorial tablet to Mozart's sister; the tomb of St. Rupert, whose bones, however, rest in the cathedral, with the exception of those that have been distributed to various churches dedicated to him; and the splendid tomb built by Wolf Dietrich for his father, Hans Werner von Raitenau, who died in Croatia. The tomb was originally in the nave. A vein of white marble in the red marble of the effigy has been used to depict a wound in the warrior's forehead received when he was fighting against the Turks.

Nearby is the Churchyard of St. Peter, a romantic cemetery right up under the rock of the Mönchsberg; and, equally near, the catacombs which were only disclosed by a landslide and part of which probably date back to the third century. I have only mentioned four of the most interesting of Salzburg's churches, but those who have time will certainly go in search of the Kajetanerkirche, which belongs now to the Hospital of the Brothers of Mercy and which with its dignified façade and lovely stucco work by the brothers Brenno deserves a visit; just as the Nonnberg Nunnery with its surviving romanesque wall paintings in the nun's choir dating from 1140 A.D., or the Erhardtskirche nearby, where again we meet the work of Francesco Brenno and whose architect, as in the case of the Kajetanerkirche, was Caspar Zugalli, who gave it in 1685 a façade that in some measure prophesies those of Fischer von Erlach. The Ursulinen-kirche is attributed to Fischer for reasons of style; both it and the Mülnerkirche have galleries which are triumphs of elaborate decoration. The pilgrimage church of Maria Plain has a façade which is a prosaic variation on the theme of the twin towers, and its high altar by an unknown Salzburg master typifies the more ostentatious and less attractive features of early baroque, pietistic rather than lyrical and flowing.

Of secular buildings in Salzburg the most famous is, of course, the castle, which dominates the whole town from its eminence on the Mönchsberg (65) and to which the easiest way to mount is by the funicular, although you will not be able to do this during the three mid-winter months. It is an original vehicle,

66   SALZBURG: Looking down on the Cathedral (*c.* 1628), and
(*right*) the tower of the Stiftskirche, from the Mönchsberg

67 Schloss Mirabell: the Ma[
Staircase (1726)

Lucas von Hildebrandt, architect;

Raphael Donner, sculptor

68 The rococo façade of
the house where Mozart
was born in 1756

economically operated by the car at the top filling its under-carriage with water so as to outweigh the one at the bottom. When it reaches the bottom the plug is pulled and you can hear the water gushing forth preparatory to the next journey. Simple as the arrangement is, two good car loads are borne aloft for 400 feet without difficulty, a mode of transport that must be nearly as cheap to run as the Danube car ferry at Melk. From the station at the top it is only a few steps to the castle entrance. Here the archbishops retired safely during the sixteenth-century peasant wars and had little to worry about, the Hohensalzburg having been made practically impregnable since its inception in 1077. Having been suitably awed by the torture chamber and impressed by the Great Horn—the Sierorbull—a monster barrel organ of 1502, with two hundred stops to peal out over the town, one should visit the Lookout Tower and the terrace, from which a magnificent view of the mountains toward Berchtesgaden can be had. Berchtesgaden was once part of the province of Salzburg. In the middle of the flat plain at the back of the Mönchsberg stands a solitary house completely cut off from even the furthest fringes of the town. It is the Hangman's House. It stands in grim isolation and its very appearance is forbidding. It has no garden. Either the Salzburg hangman was not allowed a garden or it was felt that he was the sort of person who would be unlikely to want a garden. Mrs. Van der Elst would very definitely approve both the situation and the aspect of the Henkerhaus. It is a house "to make fear".

When troubles such as the peasants' rebellion had blown over, the archbishops of Salzburg were the last people in the world to wish to remain in isolation on the top of the Mönchsberg. They were reigning sovereigns of a relatively large German state, they held court and competed to advantage with electors and princes of the other states round them. Their period of greatest magnifi-cence was under Dietrich (1587–1612), Sitticus (1612–19), Paris Lodron (1619–53), Guidobald Thun (1654–68) and Johann Ernest Thun (1687–1709). By the middle of the eighteenth century, and indeed before, the finances of the state needed more careful handling and the era of prodigality was over, a fact not without its influence on the destinies of the Mozart family. The Residenz has an architectural history covering nearly two hundred years from 1596 on. It was the archiepiscopal palace, with the courtyards of a Roman palace; just as the mews for the horses of the archbishops—now the Festspiel Haus —were ambitious. Baron Hofmann-Montanus and other leading spirits responsible for the Salzburg Festival to-day have reason to be glad that Dietrich and his successors had large ideas, perhaps not quite large enough when it comes to fitting concert audiences into the Second Winter Riding School, where you can listen to a quartet and at the same time look at frescoes of horsemen cultivating their prowess by beheading a series of busts of fierce-looking Turks. The Summer Riding School, with its arcades cut back into the living rock for the benefit of audiences at equestrian displays, has undergone conversion also, in the interests of music, and holds over fourteen hundred seats for music lovers. The Residenz has fine tapestries, wall and ceiling paintings and glazed stoves. It was in its Council Chamber that the court concerts in which Mozart figured were held.

But it is not at the Residenz but in the Mirabell gardens and at Hellbrunn that we encounter something that seems unique to Salzburg and for which it is somewhat difficult to find the right word. It is a spirit of comicality in stone, of burlesque sculpture which for me personally has very little appeal. It ranges from the extreme example of the stone dwarfs in the Mirabell gardens and the figures like the "Terrible Turk", whose inability to break a tree which has already been cut across is demonstrated for us humorously, through the semi-classical and wholly burlesque statues of Flora, Athene and Ceres at the far end of the garden and on to slightly more serious efforts like the Paris and Helen, the former holding the latter, who is looking coy although captured. Indeed, there is a distinct touch of comicality about the famous copper horse Pegasus, which was not made for the gardens but brought here from the old chapter-house horse-pond, where the Innsbruck court sculptor Kasper Graz had placed it about 1661, and perhaps its humour had something to say to this promotion. Nikolaus Pevsner in *German Baroque Sculpture* has contrasted the Flora by Ottavio Mosto (d. 1701) in the Mirabell gardens with "Venus and the Dolphin" by Beyer (1725–1806), now in the Baroque Museum in Vienna, from a private garden at Penzing. He writes: "It is hardly necessary to contrast in detail the merry coarseness of the nude of 1690 with the restrained elegance of the nude of 1770. Legs, hands, hair, nose, mouth—everything is of a different character. The form of the dolphin is a graceful accompaniment to the neo-classic posture of the slender legs and hips—Hogarth's 'line of beauty'. In Mosto's Flora, the drapery, brimful of flowers, clumsily cuts through the torso." Beyer's work is indeed beautiful, but surely Mosto's statue, which Pevsner sees as an example of German national tradition strengthened by foreign influences, is so deliberately burlesque as hardly to qualify for the comparison?

Built in 1606, remodelled in rather florid baroque under Lucas von Hildebrandt in 1721, largely destroyed by and only partly rebuilt after a fire in 1818, the Schloss Mirabell is worth visiting chiefly for the sake of Hildebrandt's staircase, down the balustrade of which slide Raphael Donner's charming *putti* (67), as well as the lavish decoration of its marble hall, two of the few things that survived the fire. The staircase is beautiful, though not to be compared with the stupendous magnificence of Neumann's staircase for the Schloss Brühl near Cologne, where the grandeur of the initial conception is reinforced by every detail of sculpture and decoration. The German princes have been reproached for the vanity which it is said led every minor princeling to attempt "a little Versailles". But unless they had possessed something of the connoisseur in their composition it is doubtful if petty rivalry alone could ever have resulted in the works of art which we now see and which were commissioned by them.

Baroque has come into its own of recent years. The courage and enthusiasm of Mr. Sacheverell Sitwell has been largely instrumental, at least in England. But there is another explanation as well—the modern photographer. Thirty or forty years ago photographers could make even the exterior of the Belvedere look deadly dull. The photograph was planned in relation to nothing except that one elementary necessity of getting the whole building into the picture, generally with a deep foreground that completely killed any individual note. This photographer of the past was a conscientious assassin of buildings. The photographer of to-day is an amiable fairy-godparent who needs watching. He—quite justifiably—composes his picture; and, sometimes, in doing so he flatters the subject. He is able to exercise a selective faculty which throws the emphasis just where it is most needed. Baroque decoration, baroque sculpture, baroque architecture stress the receding plane and also the value of light and shade in proximity. A photograph, therefore, can indicate a sculptor's intentions in the most helpful way, or, alternatively, it can soft-pedal an architect's failings. Nevertheless, the best work stands above all such strictures and needs no flattery. There are carvings in the Baroque Museum in Vienna which it would be quite impossible to flatter. I can imagine a photographer indignantly countering what has just been said, not with the old-fashioned "The camera cannot lie!"—a phrase which long ago stretched our credulity to breaking-point—but with a mild protest to the effect that all he has done is to select the most favourable angle of vision. But if favourable lighting conceals a fundamental defect the camera carries a certain responsibility, at least where the connoisseur is concerned.

There is not a great deal to attract the connoisseur at Hellbrunn, although there is plenty to keep him amused and to justify the twenty minutes' journey out by electric tram. For some obscure reason the streak of the puritan in me finds it easier to survive the notion of a Renaissance archbishop (Marcus Sitticus) with a very beautiful mistress who figures in several of the paintings, than to condone his expenditure of what must have been quite large sums of money on a series of practical jokes, involving hidden fountains and the drenching of your guests with jets of water from unexpected directions. All these toys, including some wonderful water-driven automatons, are still, after more than two hundred years, drawing bursts of delighted laughter—in which I have joined myself—from large crowds of daily visitors, and I can imagine a ten-year-old after a careful tour of all Austria giving his two hours at Hellbrunn the palm over all his other experiences. This is all right. But it is the archbishop with the mentality of a ten-year-old who paid to have them all constructed that after all this time sticks in my curmudgeonly gizzard. Even so, loyalty to him, it will be noted, has prevented me giving away any of his jokes. Go and enjoy it all and be drenched if you will, or, better still, see someone else drenched.

There is much to enjoy in Salzburg besides its superb music. There is Professor Aicher's famous Marionette Theatre at No. 15 Driefaltigkeits Gasse. There is the Glockenspiel with its entertainment of bells at seven, eleven and six o'clock from Dietrich's tower. There is the bull-organ from the castle, roaring at the beginning and ending of each of its twelve tunes. There are oddments like the Pferdeschwemme, the marble horse-pond erected in 1732 as a bathing-pool for the horses from the archbishop's stable (6); or the Marien Brunnen (fountain) and the Fisch Brunnen. There are famous men to be trailed, Paracelsus in the Pfeifer Gasse, Franz Schubert on a brief holiday at No. 8 Juden Gasse in August 1825, Hugo Wolf installed to his father's immense relief in a musical post and lodging at No. 8 Berg Strasse in 1881 (the father's relief being short-lived, Wolf and his musical director giving one another mutual notice, in a superb dead-heat, only a few months later). And, of course, there is the most famous of all Salzburg's many inhabitants, the boy child who was born on the 27th of January 1756 and christened Joannes Chrysostomus Wolfgang Theophilus (German, Gottlieb; Latin—presently preferred—Amadeus) Mozart.

Mozart is too big a subject to embark on here. He needs not a paragraph, nor a page, but a book. You can visit his birthplace at No. 9 Getreide Gasse (68) and see his first violin, the harpsichords on which he played and numerous other souvenirs of himself and of his family. In 1914 Salzburg created the Mozarteum in his honour, an academy for music at the back of the Theatre. Perhaps the shades of two much criticised individuals stood by during that opening ceremony, hoping for slightly better treatment from the orators than they have had at the hands of Mozart's biographers. Leopold Mozart adored his son and lived with one single idea, to promote his interests, but he has come in for as much hostile comment as Ruskin's adoring parents or as Anatole France's anxious and sleeplessly-devoted mother. It was a happy enough trio that toured Europe, father, son and daughter, and it is almost inconceivable that Leopold Mozart could ever have deliberately endangered his little son's health by taking him from place to place and giving him an opportunity to play for the Empress Maria Theresa and be picked up off the palace floor by the young archduchess Marie Antoinette when he fell. ("You are good. I will marry you," was the form his thanks took. And when the Empress asked him why, "She was kind to me. Her sister stood by and did nothing.") Posterity is far less interested in psychological justice than it is in legend, and just as Marie Antoinette's thoughtless "Why don't they eat cake?" has been used to make a monster of the one who rushed to the little Mozart's assistance when he fell, so the over-anxious, over-solicitous Leopold Mozart goes down to posterity as having undermined his son's health and must turn in his grave each time he hears the charge made.

The arch-criminal, however, has never been his father but his employer, so that the wicked Archbishop of Salzburg who poisoned Mozart's life by his lack of sympathy and his exacting demands is firmly established in our minds and will take some dislodging. Patrons of the arts need to watch their step lest posterity should give them a rough handling. Not many are as circumspect as Miss Harriet Weaver, who, we are told, bestowed £25,000 on James Joyce, outright, "in case I should later want to change my mind". It is not easy to whitewash the archbishop and I shall not attempt that task. Mozart was not easy to deal with: he resented a social status which other musicians accepted; he, quite understandably, resented having to wear the archbishop's livery and to be treated like a servant ("The two valets are placed at the head of the table. I have at least the honour to sit above the cooks"). But to honour genius in retrospect is one thing, and to recognise it at the outset of its struggles is another. Let those who wax most eloquent about the prince-archbishop's iniquities ask themselves how often they have gone out of their way to lift even a finger in the aid of those who practise the arts to-day. Only when a man's fame is established are the bowels of our solicitude for him immediately—and now quite unnecessarily—loosened.

The city of Salzburg has encroached upon the space which I

intended to devote to the province of Salzburg. But it is still possible to indicate some of the latter's many attractions. A few have already been indicated in connection with the Salzkammergut, for the Fuschlsee, with its steep sixteenth-century ex-hunting lodge and château-hotel, St. Gilgen, which is only about twenty miles from Salzburg city, and the Wolfgangsee, although not St. Wolfgang itself, are all in the province of Salzburg. Those who come for the music festival often stay out as far as St. Wolfgang and similar villages, where they can obtain rooms and can combine country delights with those of the concert hall and Hofmannsthal's *Jedermann* in the Domplatz. There could be few better ways, but I have heard one proprietress of a pension lament the fact that she is put to the expense of writing hundreds of letters of refusal for the festival season, for which she may be booked out more than a year ahead, whereas her rooms may be empty at other times when, for outdoor delights, the weather is possibly far more favourable. It is a case of either a feast or a famine of accommodation, and the famine—since Austrian postage must be one of the dearest in Europe—taxes not only her pen but her pocket.

At Oberndorf, eleven miles north of Salzburg, Gruber's air, "Stille Nacht, Heilige Nacht", to words by Joseph Mohr, was sung for the first time at midnight mass, Christmas 1818. It had travelled far since then. The same simple faith which inspired it inspires many of the possessions and the seasonal rituals of the province. Others suggest a pagan origin. In late February or March there is the ceremony Aperschnazzen (from the Latin *aperire*, to open). Sometimes a single farmer, sometimes groups of young men go into the fields and crack their whip lashes, whirling twelve-foot rope lashes round their heads in a rhythmic motion to finish in the same pattern and with a simultaneous resounding crack. Then they move on in silence to the next field and repeat the ritual, which was designed to drive away evil spirits and to encourage the deities of Spring to burst forth from the hard earth. April 24th is St. George's Day and the slayer of the dragon is also the protector of all peasants on horseback and of their horses. Farmers come for miles on their flower-decked horses and wind in procession to the church. On St. John's Day in June there is the carrying of the Summer Glory Poles, fir-trunks, perhaps thirty feet high, covered with elaborately patterned floral decorations. In one village more than twenty of these Glory Poles, each representing hours of loving work, may be carried in procession. They are taken to the church, reared against the ends of the pews, and, later, carried in procession again, with the priest walking behind. Those who live near to Nature and have neither ravaged nor despised her are not slow in relating her to their conception of and their relationship with God, and it is to the credit of a church that has often been accused of ''pagan'' practices that she encourages this. There can be no religion where there is no wonder, no reverence and no delight in the multiple mystery of life.

From the city of Salzburg it is only a matter of a few hours to the top of the Gaisberg, which offers a magnificent viewpoint and is as popular with skiers in winter as it is with sightseers in summer. In the northern pocket of the province, where meadows and sub-alpine flora merge into moors and heather, lie the two lakes, the Mattsee and the Wallersee. But the more likely direction for the tourist's thoughts to turn in is southward, where the railway—built in the reign of Franz Josef as an all-Austrian alternative to the shorter route from Salzburg to the Tyrol through Bavaria—follows the course of the Salzach through the Lueg Pass and on to Bischofshofen. Before the latter is reached, however, we pass Werfen with its picturesque castle perched on its hill, a castle founded in 1077, rebuilt towards the end of the sixteenth century and never taken by storm in the course of its long history. And Werfen is the starting-point for the expedition to the Eisziesenwelt, the longest of all known ice caverns, which is well worth the rather tiring expedition which a visit to it necessitates. This huge complex of passages—more than eighteen miles of them have been explored already—owes its existence to the activities of an underground stream in the Tertiary Period, a stream still visible in the shape of the most wonderful frozen waterfall in the world. The original discovery was made by a Tyrolean alpinist, Von Passelt, in 1879, who, however, found himself halted by an immense wall of ice. Only in 1913 did the spelæologist A. von Murk surmount this impediment and begin

69 Village grave-
yard at SÖLDEN in
the Ötztal

70 In the
gardens at
HELLBRUNN

71 "Schützenfeier" at ST. JOHANN IM PONGAU

72 A mountain spring at HINTERTUX

the exploration of the many caverns and passages which lay beyond. The largest of all, the Mörk-Dom, is named after him. He was killed at the age of twenty-seven in the first world war, in Galicia, but his ashes were brought here in 1925 and are deposited in a niche of the wall. In winter the air streams in through the entrance of the cavern, in summer it rushes out through it in an icy blast. This is an Aladdin's Cave of wonders which to many people will seem one of the most interesting things in the whole of the Eastern Alps. From Bischofshofen the railway continues through St. Johann im Pongau, from where one can mount to the Liechtenstein-Klamm, one of the finest ravines in the Alps, and, from a path hewn in the rock, see the swirling water descend in a series of cascades as it rushes through the narrow gorge which it has cut for itself in the rock.

Soon after St. Johann im Pongau the Tauern Railway branches off from the main line to begin its picturesque climb towards Hof Gastein and Bad Gastein. Presently it will plunge into the heart of the mountain and emerge in Carinthia. We are looking at the scenery which inspired Schubert to write his lost "Gastein Symphony", and his—fortunately not lost—seventeenth sonata in D major. He came here in a spirit of thorough holiday in 1825 on a round trip with his friend Michael Vogl the singer. The poet Grillparzer had been living in Gastein seven years before this. Both Hof Gastein in mid-valley and Bad Gastein further up, perched, as it were, in a cleft, just as the valley begins to open out, are popular resorts. Indeed Bad Gastein is a highly fashionable one, a spa with a great reputation for its thermal springs and its many excellent hotels, hotels with a long and honoured history like the Straubinger. There can be few other resorts which have a large double waterfall cutting dramatically across beneath their main thoroughfare. But this is what the waterfall at Bad Gastein does. Mountains rise on three sides, near but not oppressively so, and one sees the long procession of little silver cars mounting up the cable to the airy crest of the Stubner-Kogel, where the sun lingers long after it has left the valley below. There are delightful walks in the woods, there are cable-cars and chair-lifts for those who are in a hurry or those who prefer that the major part of their climbing should be done for them, and in winter Bad

Gastein, which gained its reputation originally as a favourite summer resort with European royalty, has become in recent years a most popular winter resort with the world at large.

Zell-am-See, which is less than ten miles beyond Bischofshofen, is another place which enjoys the benefit of a winter as well as a summer season. For those who dislike cities but who can enjoy the amenities of a smaller resort it is a simply admirable centre from which to sample some of Austria's most characteristic delights. It is on the direct route to the Grossglocknerstrasse. It is reasonably near Salzburg, near the Krimml Pass, near Bad Gastein, and connected by rail with Kitzbühel and the Tyrol. So that for those who prefer that their excursions should radiate out from a fixed centre it offers more than most places. Added to which, sleepily at ease on one side of the Zeller See and looking across a lake—on which swans slowly cruise, and a man sculls a small boat with a single spade-shaped oar—to the few châlets and the most charming alpine pastures rising behind the far bank, it is emphatically a spot to visit for its own sake. I have breakfasted in front of the Hotel Seehof in October, crossed the lake in the small motor launch which runs every two hours or so, and spent three or four blissful and solitary hours slowly ascending those pastures with no company save that of cows and grasshoppers and a very occasional child. Such hours can be more precious, to some of us, than whole days of sightseeing. Behind Zell-am-See rises the steep bulk of the Schmittenhöhe (6,560 ft.), with an aerial cable-car, holding twenty-three passengers, to take you in under a quarter of an hour to the top, if you relish being dangled in mid-air or can force yourself to endure it for the sake of magnificent skiing fields in winter, or one of the finest views in all Austria on any clear day in the year. Since I suffer from a disease which I will here and now christen appropriately telephobia, no view can ever quite counterbalance the hysteria of such moments, for while you are looking at the view you are all too conscious that you have still to face the descent. However, not one person in ten suffers from telephobia, so let the other nine go and enjoy themselves.

The trip across the Grossglocknerstrasse to the Pasterzen

Glacier and to Heiligenblut is easily undertaken from Zell-am-See. Another expedition to be undertaken is that to the Krimml Waterfalls, where a series of three falls carries the discharge from the Krimml Glacier down more than 1,200 feet and where the convenience of sightseers has been carefully studied in a series of no less than seven viewpoints.

IX

Innsbruck

ONE can go from Salzburg to Zell-am-See, and from Zell-
am-See to St. Johann im Tyrol and Kitzbühel, and on to
Innsbruck by fast electric train, a route which, although
it is making an immense detour that would shock any self-
respecting crow out of its senses (unless the crow wished to
avoid flying over Germany, just as the train is anxious to avoid
entering it), nevertheless is so pleasant and picturesque as to be
its own justification. The majority of English travellers, however, are unlikely to enter the province in this fashion, from the
north-east, and are far more likely to have come down the Inn
valley from the direction of the Vorarlberg and Switzerland.

To many English people the Tyrol is Austria and Austria is the
Tyrol. They have taken it to their heart in the same way that long
ago certain Swiss places were taken to the Anglo-Saxon heart and
have never been dislodged thence. And indeed their illusion that
"this is Austria" and that all the rest matters very little by
comparison has a certain excuse. If the federation which calls
itself the Austrian Republic were for any reason disrupted to-
morrow but the Tyrol survived intact, I believe that every
Austrian would still feel that national consciousness had its
rallying point, and that the state would be recreated one day
around this nucleus, just as Belgium was reborn from the
Ypres sector.

What is the secret of the fascination of the Tyrol? A good deal
of the credit, I believe, must go to the people themselves.
Beautiful as the scenery of the province unquestionably is, there
is nothing that cannot be equalled or perhaps surpassed in many
parts of Switzerland. But the Tyrol, plus the Tyrolese, that is a
combination which does challenge. The Tyrol is not wealthy, life
is not easy, but the people have, through the centuries, worked
out a mode of life which commands the respect and even at times
the envy of sophisticated city-dwellers. Following the stern road

of duty, they have nevertheless managed to add the virtues of gaiety, reverence and graciousness, and we feel instinctively that these people are artists in that most difficult of all arts, the art of living.

Things happen in the Tyrol that one can hardly imagine happening anywhere else. Nina Murdoch goes for a walk in the fields and at the forking of a meadow path comes across a crucifix. "There hung the martyred Christ this June morning. But on His head above the cruel thorns someone had placed a garland of meadow flowers, yellow and blue and red; and about His neck a wreath. Some child I suppose in the sunshine of the fields had been moved to weave these naïve offerings." A typically Tyrolean gesture. It is Nina Murdoch too who talks about life in the Tyrol maintaining "a fresh sweetness that has in it neither smugness nor insipidity." A good phrase that. She goes on to say: "Of all I have ever come across the Tyrolese are the only people who seem really to know the secret of weaving the philosophy of Christ into the fabric of everyday life. One feels in them serenity, brightness and strength—three splendid qualities, but arid without a fourth, the lovely one of sensibility. And that they have too. They have caught in their personality the character so mysterious and entrancing of the mountains which surround them: the luminous serenity, the strength without menace. In Tyrol I never heard a harsh raised voice nor saw a cross face, though I saw many weary ones. I used to watch the Tyrolese, wondering what could be the secret they kept that the rest of the world had forgotten or never known. And in the end I came to the conclusion their happiness was the result of their being pagan Christians—pagan in the original sense of the word. They have remained country people, closely in contact with the earth. Christ himself was pagan in that sense. He loved the countryside. In Tyrol suddenly realising that, one is more than ever astounded at the stuffiness which so-called Christians in other parts of the world have managed to impose upon His philosophy until the original shining quality of it has been lost."

As early as the eighth century Tyrol was being called "das Land im Gebirge", the Land in the Mountains. Its geographical importance was obvious to the Romans, who made it the buffer state between their empire and the territory of the Cimbri and the Alemanni. Sandwiched between the Bavarian Alps to the north and the Stubai Alps, the Tuxer Alps and the Kitzbühler Alps to the south, the province is a long narrow one, following the course of the Inn, the river entering it in the south-west corner and leaving, on its way to join the Danube, in the north-east. The Inn is an axis, west to east, with tributaries joining it at right angles from valleys which run due north or due south towards this, the main valley. And on the Inn, almost exactly half-way across the province, stands the capital, Innsbruck, with the Brenner Pass, the gateway to Italy, lying a little distance almost due south of it. The geographical outlay, it will be seen, is simple, logical and highly significant. After Innsbruck the river takes a half-turn northwards and at Kufstein, just before it leaves the province, turns directly due north.

The citizen of Innsbruck has no need to make the pious resolution "I will lift up mine eyes unto the hills", it is almost inevitable that a dozen times a day he should lift his eyes to the Nord Kette, that 7,000-foot high limestone barrier whose silver-grey ridge seems almost to touch the blue sky to the north of the city. Innsbruck seems to enjoy an almost unique relationship with the mountains. Out in the centre of its plain it looks towards mountains of varying heights all around, but has not the feeling of being dominated by any of them, not even by this immense, highly spectacular northern wall which, because the main Innsbruck street, the Maria-Theresien Strasse, lies at right angles to it, soars into our cognisance every time our footsteps are turned in that direction (79). It is like a mighty backcloth hung there to arrest our attention and at once surprise us and at the same time calm our minds with the sight of its imperturbable grandeur. Imperturbable but not inaccessible. You can live on the various terraces below its wooded flanks, with a funicular to take you home in the evenings as soon as you have crossed the river. And if you want to go higher, first one cable-car and then another will take you to the dizzy summit of the ridge, from which, if you are a fairly expert skier, you can in winter make your own descent once more to the city.

The mood of Innsbruck is different from the mood of Salzburg and to some temperaments, my own amongst them, more reassuring. It is never amusing when on solitary travel to be ill away from home. But I have taken to my bed with 'flu at the Hotel Europa, just across the square from the railway station in Innsbruck, and in this lately reborn phœnix, replacing one that had been completely wiped out by a bomb, I found not only comfort and taste and the most excellent service, all of which might be expected from a hotel which challenges comparison with the very best in Europe, but something else that one does not always expect in a great hotel, real cordiality and friendliness and understanding. Herr Direktor Hochreiter and his wife bring a Tyrolean kindliness and warmth of heart into a setting that might easily be merely cosmopolitan in different hands. But the Europa, like certain great Swiss hotels, keeps the personal touch, just as it reveals taste and craftsmanship in its furnishings and its food.

It is pleasant to praise something that is wholly new, and not solely past excellence. True, the recreated Hotel Europa has a less picturesque approach to it than the arcaded entrance in the Lauben to the Golden Rose. Nor, although it recently welcomed the King of the Belgians, can it compete with the Goldenes Adler when it comes to famous names. Paganini wrote his name on a window pane there in 1830, and Heine slept there in 1816 and Goethe in 1786 and again in 1790. Other earlier illustrious guests go right back to the sixteenth century. One could write a whole history of the hoteliers of Innsbruck. There are public records showing that the *Wirt* of the Goldenes Adler sent in a particularly modest bill when Albert V of Bavaria and his son Wilhelm, with an entourage of 400 people and 600 horses, were fêted by Archduke Ferdinand II and Philippine Welser in 1573, a contrast to the action of those other Innsbruck innkeepers who in 1518 when Maximilian was returning from the Diet in Augsburg left many of the Imperial horses and vehicles out in the street, flatly refusing to accommodate his retinue until a debt of twenty-four thousand florins owed them by the Emperor after a long sojourn in 1517 had been paid. The Emperor had told the officials of his treasury to pay;

but it had not been done then, and could not be done now, and so the burghers and innkeepers remained firm in their refusal.

Innsbruck is the city of Maximilian, well-loved by him and well loving him, even if it insulted him in this fashion shortly before his death. But it had been of importance long before he made his appearance on the human scene. The Romans had founded Veldidena where the abbey of Wilten now stands. It was the Counts of Andechs who in 1180 moved the market from the left to the right bank of the Inn and in 1239 granted the town a municipal charter. As early as 1295 Innsbruck had a banking house with a licence issued by the state, and from the middle of the thirteenth century on its importance was considerable, lying as it did on the direct trade route between the Orient, Venice and the North. The name Tyrol came from the Schloss Tirol, near Meran, which Count Meinhard gave to his wife Elizabeth, widow of the Emperor Conrad IV, and it was Meinhard's son Henry who ruled over Tyrol from 1295 to 1335 under what was really the courtesy title of King, keeping up a court of considerable magnificence and often holding jousts in the wide, level fields just outside Innsbruck and below Schloss Amras, a form of entertainment which involved him, he said, in "grozze gulte und schaden"—great expense and loss. Meinhard's daughter had married the son of the Emperor Rudolf I, thus forming the first connection with the house of Hapsburg, and his grand-daughter Margaret—who, since Henry had no son, had inherited Tirol and who has come down to us as the Ugly Duchess, or, alternatively, Pocket-mouthed Meg—eventually bequeathed the province to the Hapsburgs, thus beginning the connection with Austria. That astute family had been at some trouble to secure it. Margaret had been married in her early teens to the son of that blind King of Bohemia who was slain by the English knights at Crecy. The bridegroom at the time of the marriage had not yet celebrated his tenth birthday. Eleven years later this Prince John returned from a hunt to find the doors of the Schloss Tirol barred against him. His spouse had tired of him. The Emperor Louis the Bavarian arranged a match with his son and the marriage was solemnised by an intimidated Castle Chaplain at Schloss Tirol despite a ban laid on it by the Pope. It

198

73   The Hofburg (1755-70),
rebuilt by Maria Theresa

74   The rococo Helblinghaus,
built on the Gothic arches of
the Tauben in the Altstadt

75 Looking towards
the Goldenes Dachl,
with the wall of the
Dolomites behind

76 In the Altstadt

turned out happily, and in 1361, two years before the death of this second husband, the Pope withdrew his veto and gave the union his blessing. Margaret's later career, if legend be correct, has little to recommend it. You can see in the Ambras collection her silver drinking-cup inscribed in Gothic lettering, "Langer Liebesmangel ist meines Herzens Angel"—Lack of love is my heart's pain. But, by all accounts, she gave her heart as little pain as possible. Margaret's son Meinhard died from drinking ice-cold water when heated from dancing. He had only reigned two years. It was said that his mother had poisoned him because he had expressed disapproval of her amours. The moment news of Meinhard's death reached him in Vienna, Rudolf of Hapsburg sprang on his horse and rode through Lower Austria, Styria and the Pustertal to reach Meran, where Margaret was distributing fiefs "right and left" at the instigation of Ulrich von Matsch, one of her lovers. He hurried, and the ride took him only a fortnight. Once at Meran he persuaded his "beautiful" cousin to sign a deed making him and his two brothers her joint heirs. A few months later she abdicated and went to spend the last six years of her life in Vienna. Not for the first time, and assuredly not for the last, the Hapsburgs had seen to it that the grass did not grow under their feet.

The most interesting of the Hapsburgs to leave his mark on the Tyrol before Maximilian was Frederick with the Empty Pockets, whose pockets, by the way, were only empty when, at war with his nobles, he was being fed by his faithful peasantry. He rewarded their loyalty in 1423 when, having called the first Landtag or Parliament, with representatives of the nobles, clergy, peasantry and townsfolk, he freed the Tyrolese peasant by allowing him to bequeath or sell his farm and to change his residence at will. His successor Sigismund, nicknamed in contrast "the Wealthy"—thanks to the discovery of silver mines at Schwaz in the Unter Inntal, so that for a time Tyrol came to be known as "Silverland" and Henry VII, Henry VIII and Elizabeth I of England minted many of their coins in London from Tyrolean silver—reigned for fifty-one years. He was a jovial individual, said to have had no fewer than forty illegitimate sons, but neither his first wife nor his second gave him an heir. The first was a Scotch princess whom he married at Innsbruck in 1448. She was the daughter of James I of Scotland and sister of that Dauphiness of France who once surprised her ladies-in-waiting when she found the poet Alain Chartier asleep in a room of her palace by kissing him on the mouth and explaining that it was not the man that she kissed but the lips that had uttered so many fine sentiments. Her sister, the lovely Princess Eleanor, who married Duke Sigismund of Tyrol and who has been described as "elfin slim and supple . . . riding a-hawking in long brocaded gown with flowing sleeves fur-lined, her hair held in a golden net" in the woods of Pertisau by the Achensee, and who spent thirty-one years in the country, well liking the Tyrol and its people, but with a highly faithless husband, was also the friend of letters. She translated the romance *Ponthus et Sidoyne* from French into German and it went through a number of editions after her death. (She is misnamed in its preface "the Queen of Scotland".) In her bedroom, which you can see in just the same condition in which she left it nearly five centuries ago in the Hofburg in Meran, the Royal Arms of Scotland are beautifully carved over the doorway.

Sigismund, who had been excommunicated for years by one Pope for dealing severely with a contumacious cardinal, but completely re-established in the favour of the Church by that Pope's successor, turned devout in old age and began to endow abbeys and churches so liberally that the Landtag appointed sixteen councillors as a brake on these activities. Later the Archduke Maximilian, son of the Emperor Frederick, found this form of responsible government irksome, and in 1490 he abdicated, to devote himself to hunting and the pleasures of the table until his death in 1496 in a building erected by his father and to which Maximilian had added the Goldenes Dachl four years after the former's death.

Frederick had been popular, Sigismund had been popular, Maximilian was to be more popular still. We have reached the man whose spirit seems to brood even to-day over Innsbruck. It is still his city. Without any deliberate exploitation of the archaic, and while modern and fashionable in lots of ways, Innsbruck is nevertheless linked to the past because it has never been ashamed of the past. It sees the vanished centuries not as something alien but as something that is joined to the present by the continuity of human characteristics.

Maximilian has two memorials "for all time" in Innsbruck, the Goldenes Dachl and that stupendous tomb in which despite all the long years of elaborate preparation his body was not destined to lie. The expression "for all time" is used with due consciousness of its irony at the expense of our age. I am only too well aware of the fact that during the second world war a bomb fell within a yard or two of the heavily-protected famous balcony, which if it had fallen a second later or a second earlier would have swept the whole building away, in this case veritably "for all time". You pass down the Maria-Theresien Strasse, enter its continuation, the Herzog-Friedrich Strasse, between picturesque heavily-vaulted arcades ("Lauben"), and a few yards further on and immediately confronting you is the Goldenes Dachl, added to the façade of the Fürstenberg as a sort of royal box from which the Emperor and his court could view festivities and entertainments in the street immediately below (75). The richly-decorated late-Gothic oriel, with its steep roof tiled with more than three thousand gilded copper plates, should really be envisaged in the days of its pristine novelty, with its wall paintings fresh from the hand, it is said, of Jörg Kölderer, the court-painter (for the structure has no signature, is mentioned in no contemporary record, and would be an even greater mystery if it did not carry its date 1500 upon it), and with its carvings newly cut, probably by Erasmus Grasser of Munich. The carvings, under cover now, however, for their greater safety, represented the entertainers and the entertained, while below the lower of the two balconies were reliefs of coats-of-arms. It was a gay gesture to add these balconies and the wall paintings to the building and it is a gesture which keeps even after all these many years some of the gaiety of spirit which originally impelled it.

Within a few yards of the Goldenes Dachl, on the adjoining corner and rising out of the Gothic arches of the Lauben, is the Helblinghaus, its whole façade richly decorated in stucco—late baroque or early rococo, call it which you will—since the year 1740 a veritable sugar-cake of a house, but a most pleasing and beautiful one (74). Nearby is the Goldenes Adler, the oldest inn in the town, where Goethe, as we have noted already, slept and from the window of which Andreas Hofer addressed the citizens on August 15th, 1809. Nearby also—all of them in the Altstadt or Old Town—are the Trautson House (1541), the rather modest-looking original Rathaus, and the Stadtturm, Town Tower, reconstructed in 1560, and from the balustrade of which, reached by a fairly lengthy climb, you can view a splendid panorama of the town and its surroundings (76).

As in Salzburg, many of the buildings in Innsbruck are concentrated in quite a small area. You can do a lot of historical pottering within a relatively short time. A minute's walk takes one from the Goldenes Dachl to the Hofburg and the Hofkirche or Franciscan Church which stand, at right angles to one another, nearby. The original Hofburg was in existence here as early as 1400, but between 1754 and 1777 Maria Theresa completely rebuilt the palace, which had experienced a number of vicissitudes in the shape of fires and earthquakes (73). Apart from the decorative paintings by Maulpertsch in the Riesensaal, and some lovely old stoves, there is not a great deal to draw one to the Hofburg.

But the Hofkirche is a different matter altogether, and the discriminating will try to devote as much time as they can possibly spare to the leisurely consideration of its interior. It has been called "The Tyrolean Westminster Abbey"; and indeed if Maximilian's tomb were to-day transferred from the centre of this church to the Abbey in London it would take precedence of every monument now there. First impressions may be unfavourable and one may even feel that one has strayed into a sort of Renaissance Madame Tussaud's where the life-size figures are of bronze instead of wax and where some of the juxtapositions are, to say the least of it, curious. There they stand, this strange family assembly, in two lines either side of the massive marble sarcophagus enclosed behind its elaborate iron grille (77). They might be the automatons in the workshop of Dr. Coppelius. Everything in us that is well disposed towards classic restraint shudders at the elaborate and Gothic detail of their accoutrements until won over by the sheer integrity of the craftsmanship which it displays and by the nobility of the general conception, which in the final outcome links Gothic German art with the Renaissance. Suddenly we begin to look at them with new eyes. They command our reverence. At the end of last century the bronze figures, according to Clive Holland, "attracted the notice of but few foreign visitors", a strange commentary upon human mentality and values. To-day we gape at them as the Emperor surely intended we should gape.

He had planned a solemn procession of forty mourning ancestors to be set up in the church where his remains would rest beneath the high altar. The hands of some are extended because they were intended to contain flambeaux, to, as it were, "hold a candle" to their illustrious descendant. In 1500, when he first began to plan the tomb, Maximilian, whose armourers were un-equalled and whose foundry was turning out pieces of artillery of unique finesse, needed not craftsmen to cast the statues, but a designer to conceive them along the pattern of the Emperor's own grandiose imagination. He believed that he had found him in Gilg Sesselschreiber of Munich. The latter, however, found the taverns of Innsbruck too attractive and the girls of Innsbruck too pretty to occupy himself unduly with his task, and though the first statue was cast in 1511, the work had progressed so little by 1516 that the Emperor in a fury flung the artist into prison for a few months and then banished him to the little village of Natters, where he got down to it. You can still see his very lovely delicately-tinted pen-and-ink drawings in the Imperial Library at Vienna, with the Emperor's own unskilled suggested emendations. The Court painter Kölderer and the sculptor Magt also lent their aid, and Stefan Godl was founder. All the existent twenty-eight statues except two were cast in the foundry at Mühlau. The two exceptions were the figure of Arthur of the Round Table, there because Maximilian, who saw himself as part of the Age of Chivalry, liked to claim descent from "the parfit gentil Knight", and Theodoric, King of the Ostrogoths. These, in his disgust with Sesselschreiber, Maximilian entrusted to Peter Vischer of Nuremberg. They are said now to have been designed by Dürer, and although the upright and alert Arthur contrasts with some of the Gothic mourners I do not find them so much out of keeping with the general spirit of the work as some have claimed, nor so immeasurably superior as others have thought them. The two statues were cast in Nuremberg in 1513 and cost one thousand florins. It took them twenty years to reach Innsbruck, for Maximilian, who happened to be short of funds, pawned them to the Bishop of Augsburg, who set them up in the chapel at St. Lorenz. Ferdinand I redeemed them eventually for the amount of the original loan.

For it was his heirs who completed and set up the monument as it stands and not Maximilian. Not until 1582 was the Emperor's own statue cast. Sesselschreiber was dismissed in 1519. Maximilian, who despite the planned magnificence of his tomb had for a number of years been used to carry about with him a plain wooden coffin, of which he used to say that it was "the one narrow palace that architects can design cheaply and the building whereof does not ruin princes" (a dictum fully experienced), died at Wels in Upper Austria in 1519 and his nobles took him to his birthplace of Wiener Neustadt for burial. He had planned to outshine his ancestors in his magnificent silver armour, but the sculptor Colin has chosen to cast him in his coronation robes and the "Last of the Knights" is depicted kneeling submissively upon the sarcophagus, between the four cardinal virtues, and above those twenty-four reliefs in Carrara marble by Florian Abel which depict so graphically and with such beauty the events of the Emperor's life: his marriage with Mary of Burgundy at Ghent, his taking of Arras in 1482, his entry into Vienna after the Hungarians had evacuated it in 1490, his campaign against the Turks, and even that somewhat humiliating occasion when his daughter Margaret was returned to him and the French envoys handed over two keys, symbols of the suzerainty of Burgundy and Artois as compensation from Charles VIII for sending back Margaret and choosing to marry Anne of Brittany, whom the Emperor himself had hoped to marry.

There is much in the Hofkirche besides the great tomb in the centre of the nave which must command our interest (80, 81). The church was built in the Italian Renaissance style, to designs of Crivelli, between 1553 and 1563 and was partly remodelled in the baroque style in 1700. In the Silberne Kapelle rest the bodies of Archduke Ferdinand of Tyrol and his wife Philippine Welser, and a staircase nearby takes one up to the gallery of the Hofkirche, along the parapet of which have been placed the twenty-three smaller statues of saints which were part of the original plan for Maximilian's tomb. Of the other Innsbruck churches—some of which were severely bombed during the second world war, notably the Abbey Church of Wilten and the Servitenkirche nearly opposite the Landhaus in the Maria-Theresien Strasse—the most interesting are the Jesuit Church and the Wilten Parish Church and of course Innsbruck's own Parish Church of St. Jakob (1717–24) with its altar painting of the Virgin by Cranach the Elder and its stuccoes and ceiling paintings by the brothers Asam of Munich. Sacheverell Sitwell talks about "the multiple vocation" into which the talents of these two brothers were to pass. Both were architects and workers in stucco; the elder was a fresco painter and the younger a designer of altar pieces. There is nothing here in Innsbruck in the Pfarrkirche like the amazing stucco decorations of C. D. Asam in the little chapel of the Ursuline nuns at Straubing on the Danube, but the ceiling paintings of scenes from the life of St. Jakob are from the same hand and from the hand which painted the ceiling of the deserted Benedictine Abbey at Frauenzell, which Sitwell claims, if we except Tiepolo, "can bear comparison with any of the great painted ceilings of the Italians".

It is a mistake to regard art as necessarily the product of individualised talent. Its highest flights no doubt are linked with personal genius. But art owes much to the honest craftsman and to the fact that perhaps only from a long-standing tradition of honest craftsmen is genius able to set out for its highest flights. In Innsbruck the Gumpp family might be taken almost as the symbols of honourably practised professionalism. For about one hundred years some member of the family was court architect and they were responsible for the majority of the baroque and rococo buildings in Innsbruck. Christoph Gumpp (1600–72) built the Mariahilf Church and designed the Abbey Church in Wilten. His son, Johann Martin the Elder (1643–1729), rebuilt the Spitalkirche, into which old and young flock from the Maria-Theresien Strasse on a Sunday evening, and built the church attached to the convent of the Ursulines in the Innrain. He had two sons, Georg Anton (1682–1754) and Johann Martin the Younger (1686–1765). The plans of the former for rebuilding the Parish Church were rejected by the Emperor Karl VI as too ornate, but he was commissioned to build the Johanneskirche on the Innrain and also the new Landhaus for the Estates of Tyrol. The latter, with its fine straightforward and dignified façade, places him high in the list of architects of the baroque period. Its Diet Hall is one of the most beautiful interiors in Innsbruck and it has a fine staircase with stucco ornamentation and frescoes by C. A. Asam. Johann Martin the Younger in conjunction with Konstantin Johann Walter made the plans for the present Hofburg, the rococo palace replacing Maximilian's "New Palace". This is a mere outline of a few of the activities of this talented family.

Innsbruck has one particularly lovely fountain. It is the Leopoldsbrunnen of Kasper Graz, across the road from the Hofburg, with an equestrian statue of the Archduke Leopold V in the centre and four graceful nymphs at the four corners of the fountain basin. More memorable still—in fact, if one thinks of Innsbruck one immediately visualises them—are two monuments. The first is the Annasäule, a tall column of red marble in the centre of the Maria-Theresien Strasse crowned with a statue of the Virgin but getting its name, St. Anne's Column, from the fact that it was erected to commemorate the departure of Bavarian troops who had occupied the city for a time during the War of the Spanish Succession and who took their departure on St. Anne's Day. It is the work of Benedetti Mori, and it is no doubt one of the things that help us to lift up our eyes to the hills as we come down the Maria-Theresien Strasse towards the Lauben. The other is the triumphal arch at the south end of the same street which stands there for a double purpose—which it fulfils as deliberately as an eighteenth-century mural in an English country parish church—to commemorate the state entry of the Empress Maria Theresa and her consort Francis I into Innsbruck for the wedding of their son Leopold to the Infanta Maria Ludovica, as well as the subsequent death of the Emperor before the festivities were concluded (78). Emblems of rejoicing

77   INNSBRUCK: Bronze figures on the Tomb (1502–83) of the
Emperor Maximilian in the Hofkirche

78   The classical Triumphal Arch (1765)

79   The Maria-Theresienstrasse

INNSBRUCK

and mourning occupy opposite sides. It is intelligible that an eighteenth-century sculptor should have found the temptation to moralise irresistible; but, shorn of its garlanded urns, the arch would have, and has even now, a certain dignity.

Maria Theresa gave Tyrol a number of reforms that were long due. She abolished torture and the burning of witches. As late as 1680 thirteen unfortunates had been burnt at Meran on a charge of being in league with the Devil. She introduced a compulsory school age and peasant schools had to teach reading and writing as well as to furnish religious instruction. Her son Joseph I showed liberal tendencies not wholly approved by the religious Tyrolese, who saw the miseries of the subsequent French wars as God's judgment on the dissolution of so many monasteries by the Emperor in the ten years' course of his reign. He had closed the University of Innsbruck, which his brother Leopold II subsequently reopened. The Tyrol had escaped the ravages of the Thirty Years' War but the Counter-Reformation made itself strongly felt there and on October 28th, 1655, Queen Christina of Sweden, daughter of Gustavus Adolphus, the champion of Protestantism, delighted Innsbruck by coming to the Hofkirche in a plain black silk gown with a cross on her breast in which five great diamonds, representing the five wounds of Christ, sparkled, to abjure Protestantism and to make the Latin profession of faith after the Papal nuncio. "The Innsbruckers celebrated the event of her conversion to the true faith by the firing of cannon and the ringing of the church bells."

Innsbruck is full of the ghosts of great ones, too many to mention here. But there is one which must not be forgotten. I agree that the Hofkirche is not the place to be put in mind of that great patriot Andreas Hofer, for there can be few church statues less attractive than the one which represents him there. As Nina Murdoch inimitably puts it: "Banality had set a heavy hand upon art by Hofer's day, and the unimaginative solidity of that great figure with '1809' blazed in the centre front of a belt which of itself already draws sufficient attention to the too heroic propor-tions of the patriot's waistline, cannot be contemplated in the proper spirit with the noble perfection of Vischer's conception of Arthur of the Round Table and Theodoric of the Ostrogoths still new in the mind.'' The statue is a superb example of realism defeating its own objective, saying everything so clearly that nothing in the end is said. In fact, to our eyes to-day it is bad art at its very worst, though I must not forget that bronze group of a huntsman and two dogs which stands in front of the Kaiser Villa at Bad Ischl and which distressed me by its sentimentality, ''charmed'' a recent literary traveller who has recorded the fact as one of his most pleasurable impressions, and must have charmed its Imperial purchasers who first set it there. Perhaps the Hofer statue also has its admirers.

After Napoleon's victory at Austerlitz he handed the Tyrol over to the tender mercies of the Bavarians, and it was to free the province from this particularly galling yoke, more galling than ever because of the interference of the Bavarians in church affairs, that a national rising was planned and that the huge broad-shouldered, black-bearded innkeeper from South Tyrol made his way with two companions to Vienna to ask the support of Austrian troops and subsidies from the Archduke John. The impression made by Hofer was so favourable that the archduke chose him to head the rising. Another deputation made its way slowly to England, arriving in London in time for the Jubilee celebrations of George III. It was given a subsidy of £30,000—too late to be of use, but a gesture not forgotten by the Tyrolese even to-day. Hofer tasted success—you can see the picture of him in the Ferdinandeum, receiving the Emperor's Chain of Honour from his emissary—and for two months ruled in the Hofburg in Innsbruck as Governor of Tyrol. Then Napoleon, who had seen his Saxon and Bavarian allies out-manœuvred and out-fought by mere peasants, sent fifty thousand picked troops from Italy. Hofer was quickly defeated, made his submission to the Viceroy of Italy, dispersed his veterans and then was foolish enough to allow himself to be persuaded to resume hostilities. Within two days a price was on his head, and soon the traitor Franz Raffl had led the French to his hiding-place. His old enemy General Bisson presided over the court-martial which condemned him to be shot, and on February 20th, 1810, less than a year after those beacons had been lit on April 8th, 1809, which made ''Anno Neun'' so memorable to the Tyrolese, Hofer with unbandaged eyes faced the firing squad. He had written the night before to his friend Prueder arranging for Mass to be said for the repose of his soul, "a scrawling letter mis-spelt but serene", Nina Murdoch calls it, but its final words are to my mind tragically bitter ones: "Farewell, vile world! Death in my eyes is not worth a single tear." Yet who shall blame him for calling a world vile that had first pressed the cup of success to his lips and then so cruelly snatched it away? Fifteen years later some Tyrolese officers secretly disinterred Hofer's body from the garden of the priest in Mantua who had confessed him and brought it back to Innsbruck to be buried in the Hofkirche.

Hofer is the symbol of peasant courage and peasant virtue. The life of the people and the form of their homes have not changed so immensely since his time, and if one wants to draw still closer to them a visit to the admirable Volkskunst Museum, with its collection of peasant costumes and peasant utensils and possessions, is the obvious step to take. Both it and the Ferdinandeum or Tiroler Landesmuseum deserve their high reputation. Berg Isel (Mount Isel), rising behind the Abbey of Wilten, brings back Hofer to mind, for it was from here that he launched his successful attack on the city, a fact duly commemorated by a monument now. Igls, highly popular in summer and still more popular as a sports resort in winter, looks down on Innsbruck from the same, the south, side and from the fairly lofty slopes on which it perches a cable-car runs to the summit of the Patscherkoff, where there is an hotel and from which even finer views can be obtained.

Also overlooking Innsbruck, but lower down and further along the same slopes, the white bulk of the Castle Amras stands out unmistakably against its background of trees and green fields (95). It looks towards the city and towards the long ridge of the Nord Kette. The romantically-minded as well as the connoisseur will not fail to visit it, for it was here that Archduke Ferdinand II of Tyrol brought the beautiful Philippine Welser, daughter of an Augsburg patrician, whom he had secretly married in 1557. Legend has it that she persuaded her father-in-law the Emperor to relent and to recognise this morganatic marriage by making her way slowly to Vienna and stating a hypothetical case, only revealing her identity after he—moved by her beauty—had already given his verdict. But whether this story is true or not, she herself is far from being legend. That she was beautiful is proved not only by hearsay of the centuries but by her portraits, notably the one with the high black collar and single ruff and the exquisitely embroidered close-fitting cap. It was said of her as it was said of Mary Queen of Scots, that when she drank wine the ruby of the wine could be seen through the alabaster of her throat. She was loved by the Tyrolese for her kindness of heart and for her devotion to their welfare. The sick were her especial care and she had her own dispensary at Amras in the charge of a famous chemist Guranta, while in the Hofbibliothek in Vienna is a book of prescriptions in her own hand. Her husband, Archduke and Governor of Tyrol, was a connoisseur in more than feminine beauty. He rebuilt the castle of the Andechs completely and gave it the first monumental Renaissance hall north of the Alps, a long gallery known as the Spanish Room, built in 1570 and one of the finest examples of the German Renaissance. It precedes the town halls in both Augsburg and Nuremberg and challenges any of its successors, with its fifteen windows in the southern wall throwing abundant light on to the life-sized portraits of the rulers of Tyrol. Ferdinand made one of the most impressive collections of art of his own or any other age, numerous pictures, rare books and treasures such as Cellini's exquisite gold salt-cellar— expatiated upon at some length in his autobiography—which he made for Francis I and which the King of France gave to the art-loving Archduke. All these treasures were still at Amras in 1805 when Napoleon invaded Austria. Many of them were then moved for safety to Vienna, which explains why if we wish to see Cellini's masterpiece we must now make our way along the Ringstrasse to the Kunsthistorisches Museum instead of up the hill to Amras. The most celebrated suit of armour of all, which the Archduke ordered from Jörg Seusenhofer of Innsbruck as a present for Francis I, was for some reason never despatched to him but remained in the collection until it was stolen by Napoleon, not from Amras but from Vienna, and is now to be found in the Louvre.

80, 81   INNSBRUCK: Baroque decoration on the pulpit of the Hofkirche

82   A castle at Landeck in the Arlberg Mountains

83 KITZBÜHEL: A famous winter-sports centre, in summer

TYROLESE LANDSCAPES

84 Masked processional figures in the Festival to Welcome Spring
at IMST in the Tyrol

X

Tyrol and Vorarlberg

IF you like the Tyrol you will be well advised to devote years
to it rather than days or weeks or even months. Indeed those
who like it best are likely to begin with one particular corner
and never get much further. It endears itself to them in the way
that places in the Bernese Oberland do to the stranger and they
return again and again. It is ironical that the old capital of the
province, Meran, and the castle nearby, the Schloss Tirol, from
which the province got its name, are not part of my subject
matter here. You can search the index of any recent Baedeker, or
that of Ernst Marboe's comprehensive *Book of Austria*, for them
in vain. For they are in that part of Tyrol which was transferred
to Italy after the first world war. The castle is mentioned in
records as early as the fourth century A.D. From its rocky
eminence it looks down on Meran in the valley below, or rather
as much of it as remains does so; for in 1809 the occupying
Bavarians, with that scant sympathy that rival patriotisms show
for one another, sold the castle for a couple of hundred pounds
to a purchaser who desired its stones as building material.
Admittedly it had already fallen into grave disrepair.

The same reason which banished Meran from the Austrian
Baedeker has cut off East Tyrol from the rest of the province. To
get from Lienz to Innsbruck one must either take a trip through
Italy or else cross the Grossglockner Strasse or go by train
through the Tauern Tunnel from Spittal to Bischofshofen in the
province of Salzburg. East Tyrol is to Austria rather what the
Ticino is to Switzerland. It is, in relation to the rest of the
province, "the same and yet not the same", for its adjacency to
the Dolomites gives it a flavour of its own, and we vaguely sense,
though in less degree than in the Ticino, that Italy is not far off.
The Plöcken Pass through the Roman Lonicum (Lienz) is
believed to have been used frequently by Cæsar. In later ages it
was supplanted in favour by the Brenner, for trade naturally

tended to run north to Innsbruck rather than through Carinthia and Styria. Lienz itself is well worth a visit and could be made the centre for a delightful holiday, or can be taken *en route* to or from Carinthia. Its surroundings are beautiful, and the sight of the Unholdenscharte in the Lienz Dolomites is a memorable one. The town itself is at once quiet, friendly and alert. Its citizens give the impression of standing firmly on their own feet. It was at Lienz in the Hotel Traube that I first noticed the work of that admirable artist and craftsman Hermann Pedit, who—and it is not surprising—proved on further acquaintance to be a notability in this respect. He had won gold medals and Grand Prix in Paris and Brussels and other places far from his native town and was the same unspoilt straightforward craftsman and servant of the arts that one would expect to find in a place like Lienz, with a touch of the spirit of the mediæval guilds in his forge and workshop. Anyone who has seen one of his wrought-iron grilles will endorse this, and the same instinctive taste and mastery of the medium is evident in the delightful painted wood-carving which an elderly local carpenter has done, also for the Hotel Traube. Tyrol honours its craftsmen, gives them a living and the kind of life they like, and spares them the hardships of temptations which lead to mass production and to a speedy deterioration of standard. Appreciation and a competency are enough to save most craftsmen from prostituting their gifts. A mile or two outside Lienz is the Schloss Bruck, built by the Count of Görz-Tyrol towards the end of the thirteenth century and now converted into a museum which houses many items of considerable historical interest as well as a number of paintings by Albin Egger-Lienz— who in his later development sometimes suggests Hödler as well as other late nineteenth-century artists who made East Tyrol their terrain. East Tyrol has many relics of Roman and later ages. Native dress has as strong support here as in any part of the country. And for those who like beautiful scenery but prefer to be off the beaten track of tourism this amputated limb of the province offers as much and in some ways more than better known districts.

Not that the reputation of Kitzbühel and its Alps is in any degree exaggerated (83). Kitzbühel was well-loved by a number of nations long before the present Duke of Windsor went there in 1935 at a time when what amounted to a German ban on foreign travel had hit the place rather hard. His evinced affection gave it good publicity in Great Britain at a moment when this was most welcome to Kitzbühel's inhabitants. But the English had liked it for a number of years before this and like it better than ever to-day. It is not difficult to explain its popularity. Here we get the most friendly small town in what might be called the gentler type of Alpine scenery, absolutely ideal ground to explore in a leisurely mood in summer, or to ski over in winter. Though it has a deservedly high reputation for winter sport and is more quickly reached from England, St. Anton, with its steep slopes, expects more from its skiers, which is perhaps why its ski-school was one of the earliest and best organised in Austria. Classes are kept hard at it mastering the stem-bogen—*ad nauseam*, one almost feels inclined to say—before they are encouraged to leave the practice slopes. To be trusted on a mountain you must be capable of stemming on any slope, however steep. But at Kitzbühel there are plenty of gentle gradients as well as steep runs. It is like Saaner-Moser in the Bernese Oberland, a paradise for rabbits as well as experts. The scope of this book does not include winter sports, but since this is practically my first allusion to the subject I may perhaps be forgiven a paragraph or two now. Next to Switzerland, where, as we know, the English largely blazed their trail, Austria was the first European country to take ski racing and ski technique really seriously, and enthusiasts like Georg Bilgeri and Hannes Schneider were amongst the earliest to help to turn skiing from a sport to a science. Some of us regret that it ever did become a science, or, if that was inevitable—for when a thing is as difficult as skiing theorists spring up like mushrooms to point the way—that once having solved its more fundamental problems it did not then sit back (or even sitzmark back) and enjoy itself in a more informal and less organised fashion, instead of pressing forward towards the rigid binding and broken legs. Perhaps a high degree of organisation is inevitable the moment a sport becomes the possession of more than the happy-go-lucky few. To-day in Austria the Christmas-holiday skier—and the vast majority of visitors come under that heading—will find all his needs carefully catered for. There are chair-lifts and cable-cars and ski-hoists and every other ingenious method of avoiding having to climb a mountain before sliding down it. There are delightful small resorts and fashionable large resorts. There are excellent ski-teachers who combine efficiency with charm and humour. If anyone cares to read the later part of my book *Mount Ida* they will find there a picture of an Austrian ski-school at Kühtai (91), a remote but delightful resort above the 6,000-foot line, and some indication of its good humour and friendliness and the difference it made in the lives of its mountain guests.

Any village above 2,000 feet offers the chance of snow and winter sport in Austria. Semmering lies nearest to Vienna, if one wants to leave the capital and be certain of snow. Cable railways or cogwheel railways are to be found at Mariazell, Kanzel, Ebensee, St. Wolfgang, Zell-am-See and Bad Gastein, as well as at Innsbruck, Seefeld, Stuben, Leck (88) and other places; while ski-lifts are even more numerous. Broadly speaking the rule is the same as in Switzerland, the higher the place the greater the chance of snow in December, though the Snow Goddess can occasionally be capricious in her gifts, favouring a low altitude at a moment when another fairly adjacent high altitude has no snow at all. For the normal skier, that is to say for the one whose prowess is only indifferent, a place like Bad Aussee, with which one can quickly establish a sense of intimacy which is almost possessive, often makes for the happiest holiday. And the Austrians, naturally friendly at any time, have the gift of making their visitors feel immediately at home.

Kitzbühel, popular as it is as a winter sports resort, is far more than that (83). The village has a long history. It was given municipal rights as early as 1271 by Duke Louis I of Bavaria. Its Schloss Kapsburg was in the possession of the Counts of Lamberg for centuries, just as, with the same respect for continuity, the Stütz family, or Stitz family, have been making hats in Kitzbühel for centuries. In the Heimat Museum can be found a portrait of a member of the family who was thus occupied as early as the seventeenth century. Copper, it is believed, was mined in the district as early as 1000 B.C. In 1540 A.D. silver mines were discovered and an immediate boom resulted. One shaft was sunk to

85   A " rain-crying " festival

86   Carrying an image of the Virgin at SÖLDEN in the Ötztal

TYROLESE PROCESSIONS

87   ST. JOHANN IM TYROL

88   Coming home from church at LECK

VILLAGES OF THE TYROL

a depth of 3,150 feet, which would be impressive even to-day. At one time thousands were drawing a living from this source. In Kitzbühel the women have what is a unique privilege in Tyrol; they sit on the same side of the church as their husbands at Mass, a privilege earned for having rung the bell in the Katerinen Kirche when raiders threatened the village. An alternative version of the legend runs that they drove off the raiders with their own hands. With its lake, the Schwarzsee, considerably more attractive than its name, the Black Lake, might suggest, and with the Kitzbüheler Horn, which, apart from its usefulness to skiers, offers the most superb view to those who ascend it, Kitzbühel beguiles its visitors, who on days of procession have abundant opportunity to study the local costumes. The villagers of Westendorf, Brixen and Kirchberg have their annual *Antlassritt* on Corpus Christi, a procession on horseback to the Schweden-kapelle on the road to Kirchbichl, about an hour's walk from Kitzbühel. The chapel stands on the spot where the troops of Gustavus Adolphus were driven back by local peasantry in 1643. "Thus far and no further came the Swedish horsemen." But historians have it that no Swedish troops were ever in this part of Tyrol. The tiny chapel at a height of 6,000 feet on the rounded summit of the Hohen Salve is token of a kindred spirit of piety. It is said to have been built by a woman who sold all she possessed to place it there. Her son was a highwayman and she was convinced that he risked not only punishment in this world but eternal hell-fire in the next. She pleaded with him so eloquently that he went and gave himself up to the authorities and was duly executed, and the mother built the chapel in gratitude for his salvation from worse things.

The country round Kitzbühel is lovely, but I'm not sure that the country round St. Johann im Tyrol (87), which lies a little way up the line running across the Griessen Pass to Zell-am-See and Bischofshofen, is not equally lovely and almost more attractive to the gentle-spirited skier. There are abundant suitable slopes and they are gradual and infinitely varied, a rabbit's paradise, and after all the majority of us are rabbits on skis in the same sense that David Garnett after he had taken a course in civilian flying wrote a book which he named *A Rabbit in the Air*.

The houses here and around Kitzbühel conform to the low, broad pattern which is found also in the Lower Inntal peasant houses. Though, as in the case of Switzerland, the names of the villages and the pastures recall not one but various races, nevertheless a common mode of life has long since moulded heterogeneous elements into a corporate whole. Whatever their ancestry, the people feel themselves first of all to be Tyrolese. Piety is a strong factor in giving Tyrol its feeling of unity, as is hinted in the song which refers to the "Holy Province" of Tyrol. Dialect, dress, modes of agriculture and modes of building may vary from valley to valley, or even from village to village. In the Lower Inntal farms may be divided and several families live under one roof, even to there being four ranges in the four corners of a great kitchen. Dialect varies. Glaciers, which are *Gletscher* to townfolk, are *Ferner* to the people of the Ötztal and Kees in the Zillertal. If a man moves from his own parish even into a neighbouring one, he is an "immigrant" for the rest of his life. Life has its mould, its conventions, its gracious touches. These people have studied the art of living over the centuries. Every farm has its orchard and small garden nearby, a garden in which will be growing many of the flowers dear to the heart of the English villager, like pinks and mignonette as well as fragrant herbs. Dr. Franz Gschnitzer gives this description of the interior of a farmhouse: "On the ground floor you will find the living-room and the kitchen. The former will be panelled, and in a dark corner there will be the stone-built stove in all its snugness, whereas the large table will be standing in the window-corner. Along the walls and throughout their length there is the bench, which widens behind the stove to form the spacious stove-bench. The place is called 'Hell'! Just beside it, at least in the old farmsteads, there is the entrance to 'Heaven', that is a ladder leading up through a trap-door into the sleeping-room. When the womenfolk are climbing up the ladder the poor souls in 'Hell' may get a glimpse of 'Heaven'. Cupboards are built into the wall and the big grandfather clock is also built into the wall flush with the panelling. The little basin containing consecrated water is to the right of the door, and the crucifix, decorated with a red and yellow corn cob, is installed in the corner above the dining-table whence it blesses the daily bread. The small windows are crowded with flower-pots.''

Less than six per cent. of the area of Tyrol is arable, and in Vorarlberg the percentage is even smaller. Forests and pastures account for much of the remainder. Dairying is a major industry, and the cow, as important as she is in Switzerland, has her own ceremonial of life, the lead cow with her great bell being fully conscious that she is responsible for the behaviour of younger and more skittish companions. She will wear her decorations with bovine dignity when the herd returns to the lower pastures at the beginning of autumn. Even the goats are garlanded when they return in procession to the villages. Here as in Carinthia the draped hay poles are a feature of the landscape in late summer and I never look at them that I do not wonder why the Donegal farmer, whose hay so often rots on the ground waiting for the single fine day which might save it, has not long ago adopted a similar practice.

The Kitzbühel railway joins the main line from Innsbruck at Wörgl only eight miles from Kufstein, a pretty small town with painted houses and a gay Rathaus. It is overlooked by a fortress that once belonged to the Bavarians and was believed to be impregnable until Maximilian ordered the two largest cannons of his day, the Purlepaus and the Weckauf, to turn their attention to it. The inventor of the sewing-machine was born in this unlikely little town and has his monument here, although he died poor and unthanked in an almshouse near Vienna, having benefited not at all from his ingenuity.

A few miles west of Kufstein beyond the crags of the Kaiser Gebirge is Thiersee, a hamlet on the edge of a sapphire lake with a white church pointing a slender finger towards the sky. Small country churches in Austria would make a beguiling book in themselves. They have the same sense of the dramatic possibilities in landscape which temples in Greece have, and it is doubtful if it was solely motives of prudence which drove them to the top of eminences, like that highly picturesque little church at Arzl near Innsbruck, or made so many of them all over the country white beacons in a green setting.

Following the valley of the Inn from Kufstein back through

Wörgl we should try to make time to see the curious church of St. Leonard auf der Wiese (St. Leonard in the Meadow) at Kundl, a small village four miles south-west from Wögl. It was consecrated by Pope Benedict VIII in 1020, but its wooden portal dates from the first half of the seventeenth century and is a good example of what is known as Knorpelwerk, a typical baroque ornamental motif. The church stands at a spot where a jibbing horse is said to have reminded Henry II, Duke of Bavaria, of a vow he had made but not fulfilled.

The Duke of Bavaria held Rattenberg in fief from the Bishops of Regensburg until 1505, when Maximilian added it to his Countship of Tyrol. The town is right on the bank of the swiftly-flowing Inn. As in the case of Schwaz and Jenbach its prosperity was linked with the mining industry and the variety and independence of design of its many old houses remain as a witness to that former prosperity. The Gasthaus Traube in the Klostergasse, with its quaint small turrets and its open stone staircase, gives an excellent idea of Gothic house architecture. For those who like old towns Rattenberg is what might be termed a collector's piece.

Jenbach has not any very great intrinsic interest, although it is the starting point for various excursions of great interest. But there is a wealth of historical inference in the name of one of its buildings, a building which was formerly the inn. The Alte Toleranz (it has a successor, the present Hotel Toleranz) commemorates tolerance in a rather ironic form. At the very moment when Joseph II was pressing his reforms the Tyrolese Landtag decided that what their province needed was religious uniformity, and the Protestant inhabitants of the Zillertal were asked to find a refuge elsewhere. This they eventually found in Prussian Silesia, where the village which they founded is named Zillertal. But while looking round for a new home they were permitted to stay in the inn at Jenbach, which thus acquired its name Toleranz, a name which many will think scarcely deserved in view of all the circumstances.

Two miles east of Jenbach the Zillertal opens to the south. It is a pastural valley between wooded slopes, but at Mayrhofen the main valley divides into a number of mountain gorges which lead up to the glaciers of the Zillertaler Alps (96). The district is a paradise not merely for summer pedestrians who enjoy a gentle walk amid picturesque and bucolic surroundings, but for serious alpinists and for hunters, for there are abundant chamois and deer. This is *le vrai Tyrol*. I remember being told by the poet Dallas Kenmare how she had enjoyed the activities of a local band at Mayrhofen which arrived to play in the square on a Saturday night with a repertoire of Strauss waltzes, folk tunes and excerpts from the operas and who, to her intense disappointment, departed again on Sunday afternoon, the players splendidly arrayed in large black beaver hats, navy blue braided tunics, knee breeches and white stockings. This is Tyrol not only as the visitor expects it to be but as it actually is.

The miniature-gauge railway has come to Mayrhofen from Zell-am-Ziller five miles down the valley, another picturesque resort. From here a road branches off over the Gerlos Pass to Krimml, a favourite route in olden times for travellers in a hurry to get from Salzburg and Southern Germany to Italy quickly. It must have been an undertaking then, and the road to-day has many dramatic hairpin bends: after passing through vast fir-forests and edging precipices it begins its steep descent to Neukirchen.

Jenbach is the junction not only for the Zillertal but also for the Achensee, the most admired of all Austria's many lakes. I am not sure myself that this invidious distinction should be made in its favour. Beautiful as the six miles of the Achensee are, there may be some like myself that prefer a gentle foreshore like that of the Wörthersee, and a pastural background, to anything which steep, tree-covered slopes or crags and precipices have to offer. A cogwheel railway mounts from Jenbach and a lake steamer will take you, in summer, to Pertisau, which lies on the west bank about a third of the way down the lake, magnificently situated at the mouth of the Karwendel valleys. It is easy to understand Pertisau's popularity to-day, but its popularity is far older than that. It was Duke Sigismund who, having decided to build himself a great fishing-lodge here, laid the foundations of the Fürstenhaus. Here he came with his talented and lovely Scottish wife Eleanor and here she would ride in the early morning with her falcon upon her wrist, for she loved hawking. Here no doubt also she worked on her translation of *Ponthus et Sidoyne* while her husband pursued chamois or like his successor Maximilian got himself into perilous positions from which he could only be extricated with local aid, the while his retinue prayed zealously for his safety. Maximilian has been reproached in that a picture in his fishing book in the Hofbibliotek in Vienna shows his courtiers indulging in the unsportsmanlike behaviour of netting the lake, but the Duke himself has an alibi, for he is shown perched upon a dizzy pinnacle of rock from which he is taking aim with a musket at his favourite quarry. He was an insatiable huntsman, entertaining the ambassadors of Spain and Venice on the shores of the Achensee with a strenuous day's hunting followed by a superb banquet. Seventeen years later, struck down with a fever at Innsbruck, Maximilian had himself brought by boat down the Inn that he might gaze for the last time on the mountain slopes where he had so much happiness. The Achensee has its memories also of Philippine Welser, for her husband, Ferdinand II, besides building himself a great hunting-lodge near Pertisau, had a magnificent barge made for his wife in which she and her ladies-in-waiting could drift at their ease on the lake. One further association of this place which has so many —just before revolution raised its head in 1848 and his uncle abdicated in his favour, that quite insatiable and, by comparison, relatively "modern" sportsman, the future Emperor Franz Josef, came here as a boy of sixteen or seventeen years old and stayed with Count Enzenberg in his castle at Tratzberg in order to stalk chamois on the Karwendel mountains.

The Schloss Tratzberg can be reached easily from Jenbach or from Schwaz, a town once enriched by its silver and copper mines and made notable now by its parish church, with its two naves, each with its own aisles and high altar—the explanation of the second nave, it is said, being to allow the Miners' Guild to worship apart from the townsmen—as well as its Gothic statues of St. Anne, St. Elisabeth and St. Ursula and its sixteenth-century tomb to Haus Dreyling by Colin. This piece of monumental ironwork was cast in the Löffler foundry in Mühlau, where also was cast the four-and-a-half ton bell which swings in the belfry. The roof of the church is of copper tiles, fifteen thousand of them, with a rich patina, the kind of thing that one expects in Copenhagen. In 1521 the first book printers in the Tyrol established themselves in Schwaz, which was at that time almost a rival to Innsbruck. It was from the mines round Schwaz that the Fugger family from Augsburg derived most of their wealth towards the end of the fifteenth century, and they are connected not only with the great house, four storeys high, which dominates the town square, but also with the Schloss Tratzberg, where their coat-of-arms is to be found on the panelling of the room which bears their name and where their taste was probably responsible for the beautiful Renaissance decoration of what is known as the Queen's Room. The castle has a long history going back to 1120. Perched on its rock on the far side of the Inn it was originally a stronghold in the possession of the Rottenburg family, those robber knights whose own ancestral castle is not far away across the valley. It was the wealthy mine-owner Veit Jacob Tänzel who converted it from what was a fastness into what is almost a palace in blended late Gothic and Renaissance styles, an architectural triumph which no doubt contributed a share to its remaining inhabited long after many of its contemporaries had either become museums or ruins. To-day it is still full of beautiful things, including the famous frescoed Hapsburg Family Tree in honour of Maximilian, who stayed here frequently on hunting expeditions and who is said to have chalked upon the wall of his bedroom— left as he last inhabited it with a plain wooden bench round the wall, a chandelier of stags' antlers and a bed so short that it must have brought his knees up to his chin—the following sudden excursion into introversion upon the part of a natural extrovert:

> I live I know not how long,
> I die I know not when,
> Must go I know not whither;
> I wonder that I so joyful be.

On the opposite side of the Inn, dominating Schwaz at its feet, is the Schloss Freundsberg, an example of the purely utilitarian stronghold which Tratzberg doubtless once was. Tratzberg was turned into a relatively comfortable residence for people who took a real delight in artistic things and were even aware of the advantage of washstands. Freundsberg, with its romanesque fortified tower, was an abode for fighters who realised the precariousness of existence, and though it may have looked less cheerless in former times than it does now it is easy to see that it never underwent any adaptations in Renaissance times.

Passing through Volders with its curious church (90), we reach Hall-im-Tyrol, which ranked as a town as early as 1303. Its mines—which are salt mines—have proved a more lasting source of revenue to it than the copper and silver deposits in the Falkenstein which enriched Schwaz. Salt-mining is still carried out nearby, and as its alternative name Solbad Hall suggests, the town has established its claim to being a spa. Hall was once a walled-in city with nine gates. Only one of these survives to-day, the Münzertor (89). Near to it stands the Münzerturm, a curiously shaped round tower which was part of the Castle Hasegg, which itself was part of the fortifications of the town. The Münzerturm, Minting Tower, was producing coins for Sigismund (the Rich) in 1477 and was put into commission again at Andreas Hofer's direction during his few months of triumph in 1809.

Passing Castle Amras (95) above us on our left we reach Innsbruck once more. Now is our moment to turn south to the Brenner if we wish to see the lowest pass leading south–north through the Alps which was probably known as a saddle path long before Septimus Severus built a Roman road across it. Lying in the fertile middle belt of the province, the valleys which flow out towards Innsbruck have a population of well-to-do farmers. In the Wipptal, the Stubaital and the Innsbruck basin itself, terraces called the "Mittelgebirge" have formed at a height of from 600 to 900 feet. Sometimes these terraces are wider than the valley itself. Buses run out from Innsbruck and you can enjoy the beauty of the Stubaital for a whole long day, and then, if you choose, return to the city in the evening. Another bus runs to Sellrain and on to Gries and from there you

89 HALL-IM-TYROL: The medieval Münzertor (Minting Tower)

90   The church at Volders

91   At Kühtai

<small>IN THE TYROL</small>

92   A church near Biberwier

93   Painted walls on an old inn in the Ötztal

IN THE TYROL

94 Fernstein, built
originally in the
thirteenth century

95 Amras, re-
built 1564–67
from an original
Gothic castle

can begin the climb to what used to be Maximilian's hunting-lodge and is now the Alpengasthof at Kühtai. I have described Kühtai (91) in such detail in *Mount Ida* that I shall not attempt to epitomise that description here.

Easily reached from Innsbruck by car, but deserving a great deal more than the cursory attention of a day excursionist, is Seefeld, which lies north of the Inn on the plateau of the watershed between the Inn and the Isar. Seefeld is the kind of place that invites not a night's residence nor a week's residence but a whole year's residence to watch the seasons come and go. In the autumn when its throng of summer visitors has departed, Seefeld, which spreads itself over the wide floor of the plateau, respecting the right of each house or châlet to have its own uninterrupted view of green pasturage, is gloriously peaceful. At a small hotel like the Tyrol, with its charming individual note, I can imagine the weeks going by with a visitor unable to tear himself away from a place where the air is larch-sweetened and the people are so pleasant. There is nothing claustrophobic about Seefeld; one lives as it were on a little private plain with the hills to climb and mountains to gaze at and all the cares of the world far, far distant.

The visitor who ascends the Ötztal, which runs due south of the Inn after Stams and Sitz have been passed in order to reach Ötz and Sölden or to press on to Vent or Obergurgl on the very edge of the glacier, is likely, at least in winter, to be made of sterner stuff than the kind who, like myself, might dream away days at Seefeld. The main valley has great beauty and the last three places named are excellent for skiing, and high enough to be fairly certain of snow, although the wind can occasionally blow cold off the glacier in mid-winter, whereas in spring a place like Vent comes into its own. Obergurgl at 6,350 feet is the highest parish village in Austria.

At Stams we should pause to visit the great Cistercian Abbey, founded in 1272, whose church was the burial place of the earlier Counts of Tyrol until in 1552 the mercenaries of the Elector of Saxony, returning from Innsbruck slightly soured by the failure of their attempts to capture the Emperor Charles V, broke open the graves in the nave of the church and strewed the

19*   237

bones over the fields. They had previously threatened the monks, raided their wine-cellars and trampled the Host underfoot. In a few hours they wreaked havoc. Founded by Elizabeth, widow of the Emperor Konrad IV and later wife of Meinhard, Count of Görz and Tyrol, in memory of her son Konradin, the last of his line, who was beheaded at Naples in 1268, the abbey was well endowed and owned great game preserves, an amenity of which the Emperor Maximilian liked to avail himself. But by 1593, when a severe fire broke out, the abbey was less wealthy and the monks had to wait a number of years before attempting reconstruction. The present abbey is the work of Georg Anton Gumpp of Innsbruck. In the abbot's residence, with its two red turrets, is the superb staircase with its grille and wrought-iron balustrade leading to a library which is full of treasures. The abbey has some of the finest wrought-iron work in Tyrol, and that is saying much. Leading to the small chapel adjoining the Italianate Abbey Church is the magnificent wrought-iron screen, the Rosengitter (Railing of Roses) by Bachnetzer. In the church itself over the doorway to the princes' tombs is a crucifix which is the master-piece of the Tyrolese carver Andrä Thamasch (1639–97), and the high altar carved by Steinle aus Weilheim (1609), as well as the Tomb of the Princes (1670), should all be seen.

Although it is a useful centre, affording access, for example, to the picturesque Fernstein Castle (94), a thirteenth-century mediæval fort set to guard the Fern pass, as well as to the Sigismundsberg Castle, built on a lake island in the Fernsee in 1460 as a hunting-lodge, and to Bieberwier nearby, there is little to delay the sightseer in Imst itself. Its ancient patrician houses vanished when, on May 7th, 1822, a fire burnt almost the whole town completely to the ground, only four houses surviving out of more than two hundred. Imst has a link with seventeenth- and eighteenth-century England, Russia and other countries in—of all strange things on earth—canaries. The industry was important enough for Imst traders to have a shop at Moorfield Square in London. Was it some Austrian eccentric, some ornithological enthusiast, who began breeding canaries and was so successful that presently his neighbours were infected with a kindred enthusiasm? Or had the Imst climate, despite its winter, some favourable effect on singing capacities? One can imagine a snobbishly-minded canary hanging in Mrs. Siddons' window in London remarking airily to a friend, "Of course we came from Madeira originally, in the *Mayflower*, but our family has been settled in Imst now for several generations." Did Addison when he passed this way to get from Switzerland to Italy via the Brenner in 1702 rouse himself sufficiently from some literary reverie to hear the Imst canaries? Goldsmith would have been more likely to have been fascinated by them. One can imagine him peering across the curtains of some window to discover a particularly good songster, and since Goldsmith rambled about Carinthia, it is just possible that he may have peered in Imst on his way there. The British writer who has left us some record of Tyrol is Fynes Moryson, a Scots law student at Cambridge who as early as 1595 set out on a tour of Europe, stopping at university towns in winter and resuming his tour in summer. He travelled cheaply, put up at small wayside inns, and so could study local modes of living. He kept his journal in Latin for his own edification, but in 1617 an English translation of it was published. Landeck, dominated by its picturesque castle (82), stands amidst scenery that is typical of this part of the Tyrol. Seeing it one is not surprised that the province has had many devotees.

Ruskin loved the Tyrol and has a number of references to it in his writings. On a journey with his parents as early as 1835 he travelled from Chamouni (*sic.*) to Venice via north Switzerland, Tyrol and Stelvio. Perhaps his admiration for its people dated from them. Nearly half a century later I find him writing in a letter in *Fors Clavigera*: "among virtuous nations, or the portions of them which remain virtuous, as the Tyrolese and Bavarian peasants, the Tuscans and the mountain and sea-shore races of France, England, Scotland and Ireland, almost everybody is 'well-bred', and the girlish beauty is universal." Twelve years before this he had used the Tyrolese peasant to point his moral against steam ploughs and such atrocities. "Farm after farm I can show you in Bavaria, Switzerland, the Tyrol and such other places, where men and women are perfectly happy and good without any iron servants"; and, a few weeks later, "my beau-ideal is not taken from 'a mechanical point of view', but is one already realised."

(He had promised the English a plan which would make them "round and merry, instead of flat and sulky".) "I saw last summer, in the flesh, as round and merry a person as I ever desire to see. He was tidily dressed—not in brown rags, but in green velveteen; he wore a jaunty hat, with a feather in it, a little on one side; he was not drunk, but the effervescence of his shrewd good-humour filled the room all about him, and he could sing like a robin. . . . This merry round person was a Tyrolese peasant; and I hold it an entirely practical proceeding, since I find my idea of felicity actually produced in the Tyrol, to set about the production of it here, on Tyrolese principles; which, you will find, on inquiry, have not hitherto implied the employment of steam. . . . But they do imply labour of hands on pure earth and in fresh air. They do imply obedience to government which endeavours to be just, and faith in a religion* which endeavours to be moral, and they result in strength of limbs, clearness of throats, roundness of waists, and pretty jackets and still prettier corsets to fit them."

We have reached St. Anton at the entrance to the Arlberg Tunnel, which is the boundary between Tyrol and Vorarlberg. A number of years ago St. Anton was my introduction to Austria, and I remember with what delight I sat in the sun and ate my lunch up at the Ulmer Hütte above St. Christoph for the first time, gazing down across wide expanses of perfect powder snow through which my skis would presently cut their track. The Hospice of St. Christoph, that stark, solitary building in its high valley, was founded in 1385 by Henry the Foundling, who wandered Europe before being in a position to fulfil the vow he had made as a child tending his master's cattle, that he would build a refuge for travellers on the Pass where many in those days used to lose their lives from exposure. For its support Henry founded a Brotherhood which twenty years later numbered four dukes, sixteen reigning princes and thirty bishops and abbots amongst its supporting membership of nine hundred. Few of

---

* He adds a footnote to say that he uses this term "impartially of all forms of submission to a Supreme Being adopted by men; and that such submission involving moral obligation is stated to be essential to all healthy human action".

those who ski down to the hospice to-day take the trouble, I imagine, to visualise it in those far-off pre-skiing days. As for St. Anton itself, its main street is thronged with happy skiers whose thoughts are not unduly occupied with avalanches and death from exposure. Indeed here, as elsewhere in Austria, the authorities have difficulty in getting their warnings about weather conditions taken sufficiently seriously by the visitor. Mürren in Switzerland and St. Anton-am-Arlberg in Austria are possibly the two places which have contributed most to the history of skiing as a sport, to date. I am bound to say that I think the famous ski-school of Hannes Schneider, with its insistence on "the Arlberg crouch", changed skiing from something that was lovely to watch, if dangerous to undertake, to a "safety first" hideousness from which it has never recovered, and deprived us as well of one of the pleasantest of all turns to watch, the telemark. Still, hundreds of thousands of skiers have reason to be grateful to Schneider, and everyone must admire the moral courage which led to his speedy imprisonment and then banishment by the Nazis and made Arnold Lunn promptly cancel the Arlberg-Kandahar race despite all pleas and protests.

We pass through the Arlberg Tunnel, emerge at Langen and find ourselves in Vorarlberg. It is in several respects unique. The present Austrian republic may be called a Danube state in that ninety-five per cent. of the waters of the country flow ultimately into the Danube. Vorarlberg, on the contrary, is a Rhine province and its rivers are destined to empty themselves in the North Sea. Although it is the smallest Austrian province it has the largest share of Austria's extra-territorial frontiers, for eighty per cent. of the province borders on either Switzerland, Bavaria or Liechtenstein, the remaining fifth being Vorarlberg's mountainous link with the Tyrol, which must be reached either by tunnel or mountain pass. To those coming from Switzerland Vorarlberg is the threshold of Austria, but there is very little to distinguish it from, say, parts of St. Gall, which canton lies just a little further round the south bank of Lake Constance. Indeed, there was some talk of amalgamation with Switzerland after the first world war which came to nothing, Swiss caution, if nothing else, being against it.

In the Vorarlberg, landscape, style of houses, people, culture and economy are all individual as compared with the rest of Austria. The people, largely of Alemanic origin, are a mosaic of different races, moulded in the course of time into a sturdy unity. The Romans arrived fifteen years after the Emperor Augustus ascended the throne. In parts of the province a dialect similar to the Romansch of the Grisons is spoken. In 1363 the House of Austria acquired a small estate near Götzis, its first possession in Vorarlberg and the beginning of a long process. Bregenz, the capital of the province, which was the Brigantium of Roman times, lies on the eastern bay of Lake Constance, and has always been at the cross-roads of important highways, but it remains quite a small town with twenty thousand inhabitants; Dornbirn has only one thousand more and Feldkirch comes next with sixteen thousand. This is not a province of cities, or of large towns, but of relatively small communities of between two thousand and five thousand inhabitants. Nevertheless Vorarlberg is twice as densely populated as the Tyrol. Like the canton of St. Gall, indeed possibly at one time influenced by it in this respect —or did the tide flow the other way?—it has its own flourishing textile and embroidery industry founded long ago on the initiative of individuals and of individual families, and still remaining in the hands of those families. It has a thriving cotton industry, producing multi-coloured woven cloth, and various other textile factories, only four of which in the whole province employ more than five hundred persons. The development of hydro-electric power resources has helped industry, and in all this one sees, possibly exaggerated, the influence and example of Switzerland.

In no other Austrian province is there greater attachment to local custom and local costume. There is nothing self-conscious, nothing staged, about this addiction, and the tradition here is probably unbroken, not a reaction from a late nineteenth-century lapse as it is in some places. As in Brittany, it was not necessary to create a revival, the costumes had never lost their popularity. This is not surprising when one sees how beautiful, how quaint and how individual many of them are. Never was there better reason for preserving the treasured past.

One of the pleasantest ways to arrive in Vorarlberg is to cross Lake Constance or to come down the whole length of the lake by steamer and to land at Bregenz. The huge, sleepy lake, stretching away into the distance, with its flat foreshore against a distant background of hills and mountains, always suggests Italy to me, rather than Switzerland, Germany or Austria. It is too peaceful, too serene, too much suggestive of being the gateway to a land of happy lotus-eaters (actually of thriving, hardworking farmers!) to call up the memory of days when bombs meant to be dumped one side were dropped by some confused airmen on the other. Bregenz values its lakeside situation. When in 1946 it decided to imitate Salzburg and to have its own annual festival it was the lake which was made the scene of that festival. Elaborate performances were produced on specially built island-stages on the lake to audiences that were seated along the shore. It was found that acoustics were best if the stage islands were placed at a rather greater distance from the shore, since the sound of the voices carried best over intervening water. Mozart's *Bastien and Bastienne* was produced on the water and the Vienna Symphony Orchestra gave two orchestral concerts, under Hans Swarowsky. When Mozart's *Il Seraglio* was staged on a later occasion Belmonte entered the stage from a boat and Selim Bassa arrived on what might almost have been termed a luxury ship. Max Roethlisberger of the Zürich Theater has produced Johann Strauss's *Thousand and One Nights* (on six fixed and three movable stage islands with boats moving between!). The Vienna Burgtheater gave a performance of Grillparzer's *Media*, to the huge delight of numerous German and Swiss guests, and by now singers and even ballet dancers are becoming thoroughly at home on the lake.

Bregenz has another amenity as well as Lake Constance, for immediately behind the town the Pfaender peak rises to a height of 3,500 feet, with a cable-car to take up those in search of a magnificent view to its summit. One looks over the tree-tops to that vast expanse of water which stretches away into the distance, and to the Swabian Plain, while in the near distance are the Swiss and Vorarlberg mountains. The Bregenz Wood, as it is called, begins with the Vorderwald, north of the river Ache, and is a term used to describe all the territory leading from the high plains of the Allgau to the mountains proper of the Lechtaler Alps. This so-called wood has peaks well over 8,000 feet high. At the foot of the Hochaelpele near the village of Schwarzenberg is the great wide-eaved wooden châlet which was once the home of Angelica Kauffmann, who has painted frescoes in the church nearby. Vorarlberg had its baroque architects, Thumb, Beer and Mossbrugger amongst them, but some of their best work was done outside the province, in neighbouring Swiss and south German areas, for example the Abbey of Einsiedeln, the Münster of St. Gall and the lovely baroque churches at Weingarten and Birnau.

Dornbirn lies to the south of Bregenz. Although it is a centre of industrial activity it has managed to earn for itself the title of Garden City. Its position favours it, for it is quite near the highly attractive winter sports centre of Bödele; but what has really saved it most of all is the fact that the labourers in its factories have never cut themselves off from the peasants' world from which they came and still feel themselves a part of it. Dornbirn is the starting point for most of the bus routes into the Bregenz Wood, as well as for a visit to the Rappenloch Gorge, which has been made accessible by a specially built route and which lies on the way to the health resort of Ebuit. From the Kummenberg, which rises from the midst of the plain, a fine view can be had of the Rhine valley. Götzis lies to the east, with its massive ruined castle of Neu-Montfort, a contrast to the relatively well preserved Glopper Castle near Hohenems, where the two Nibelungen Song manuscripts were found, and Schattenburg Castle at Feldkirch, which was the seat of the Counts of Montfort during the thirteenth and fourteenth centuries. To the south of the Kummenberg, branching off from the main Rhine valley, is a sub-valley which is known as the Garden of Vorarlberg, its chief town Rankweil being the most popular pilgrimage centre of this Catholic province. The double-towered Liebfrauenkirche, or Church of Our Dear Lady, stands on a rock looking out across the plain towards the mountains and deserves the title of a fortified church; its earliest parts date from the fifteenth century and it probably stands on the site of a former Merovingian castle.

96   Looking towards the Zillertal Glacier

97, 98 The village band heads
a Wedding Procession at ALPACH
near INNSBRUCK

Feldkirch, further south, is even more picturesquely situated, with the tree-covered rocks rising sheer behind the Schattenberg. Although it lies on a main east–west rail route it has kept much of its character of a mediæval township. First it was known as the "Officers' Township", then, from its grammar school and famous Jesuit college "Stella Matutine", as the Studierstädtlein or "Students' Township", but neither name is particularly appropriate to-day. The round Cats Tower rises above the trees and the old patrician houses. Like Bregenz, Feldkirch was part of the Montfort property.

From Bludenz, which afforded Frederick of the Empty Pockets sanctuary when the Emperor outlawed him, the valleys radiate out in star pattern; the Klostertal, the Montafon valley, the Brandnertal and the Greater Walsertal all terminate near this town, which has been called the "Gate to the Alps". Beautiful as the scenery of the Walser valley is, only the most expert driver should attempt to drive the valley's full length. It is a test not only of skill but of nerve. The Montafon valley is worth visiting not only for its own sake but to see Schruns, its chief town, and still more Gargellen, nestling under the massive rock formation of the Madrisa and separated from Davos in Switzerland only by the main crest of the mountain range.

From Bludenz the main line runs through beautiful scenery to Langen at the entrance to the Arlberg Tunnel. Ober-Lech, Lech and Zurs are all reached via the Flexenstrasse from Stuben above Langen. The Flexenstrasse, a fine feat of engineering, is a partly arcaded road cut into the rocky flank of the mountain. I remember skiing down it years ago from Zurs alone, after heavy snowfalls, and with snow still falling, and feeling distinctly grateful for the periodic tunnels and stretches of road-roofing which were there so that I should not find myself suddenly swept away by a small avalanche. Zurs, like Kühtai, is not a village, it is simply a group of less than half a dozen excellent hotels standing in the centre of a high mountain valley and surrounded by terrain which looks— and is—a skier's paradise. Lech, which lies beyond it and is not quite so high, is more homely and, some think, even more beautiful. Unlike Zurs, it has a pre-skiing history, demonstrated by its small church with its strongly built, square, attached tower. Nave and tower—apart from its onion-shaped baroque cupola—date from the fourteenth century. In this remote spot, cut off, it might seem, from the whole world, but where men have been worshipping God for centuries, I end this book whose peregrinations began in Vienna. This is as much Austria as Schönbrunn itself, indeed it is more so, for without the established lives of generations of peasant farmers on the plains and in the mountain valleys of Austria, Schönbrunn and all its glories could never have been.

MAPS

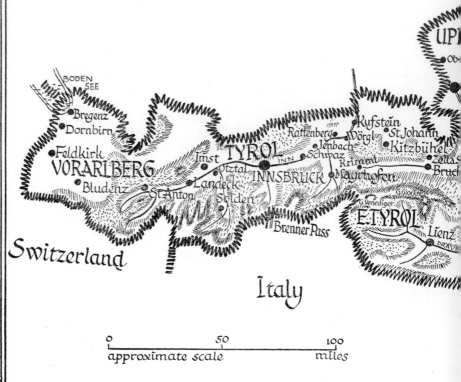

AUSTRIA

Germany

UP

Ob-

BODEN SEE

Bregenz
Dornbirn

Kufstein
Rattenberg · Wörgl · St.Johann
Jenbach · Kitzbühel
Feldkirk · Imst · TYROL · Schwaz · Zells
VORARLBERG · Ötztal · INN · Kru · Bruc
Bludenz · St.Anton · Landeck · INNSBRUCK · Mayrhofen
Sölden · G.Glock
G.Venediger · E.TYROL
Switzerland · Brenner Pass · Lienz
PRKVE

Italy

0   50   100
approximate scale   miles

Czechoslovakia
Heidenreichstein
Waidhofen
Gmünd
Zwettl
Horn
Altenburg
Mistelbach
Aigen
LOWER AUSTRIA
Dürnstein
Krems
Spitz
Göttweig
Ried
LINZ
DANUBE
Melk
AUSTRIA
St Florian
Amstetten
VIENNA
Kremsmunster
St Pölten
NEUSIEDLER SEE
Gmünden
Steyr
YBBS
Waidhofen
Lillenfeld
Eisenstadt
ATTER SEE
TRAUN SEE
Mariazell
Wr Neustadt
Ischl
ENNS
Aussee
Admont
Semmering
Hallstatt
Selzthal
Spital
DACHSTEIN
Radstadt
Leoben
Bruck
BURGENLAND
Pöllau
STYRIA
Hungary
GRAZ
Friesach
Gurk
Wolfsberg
Milstatter See
MUR
K.A.L.
Velden
Klagenfurt
Villach
Wörther See
Yugoslavia

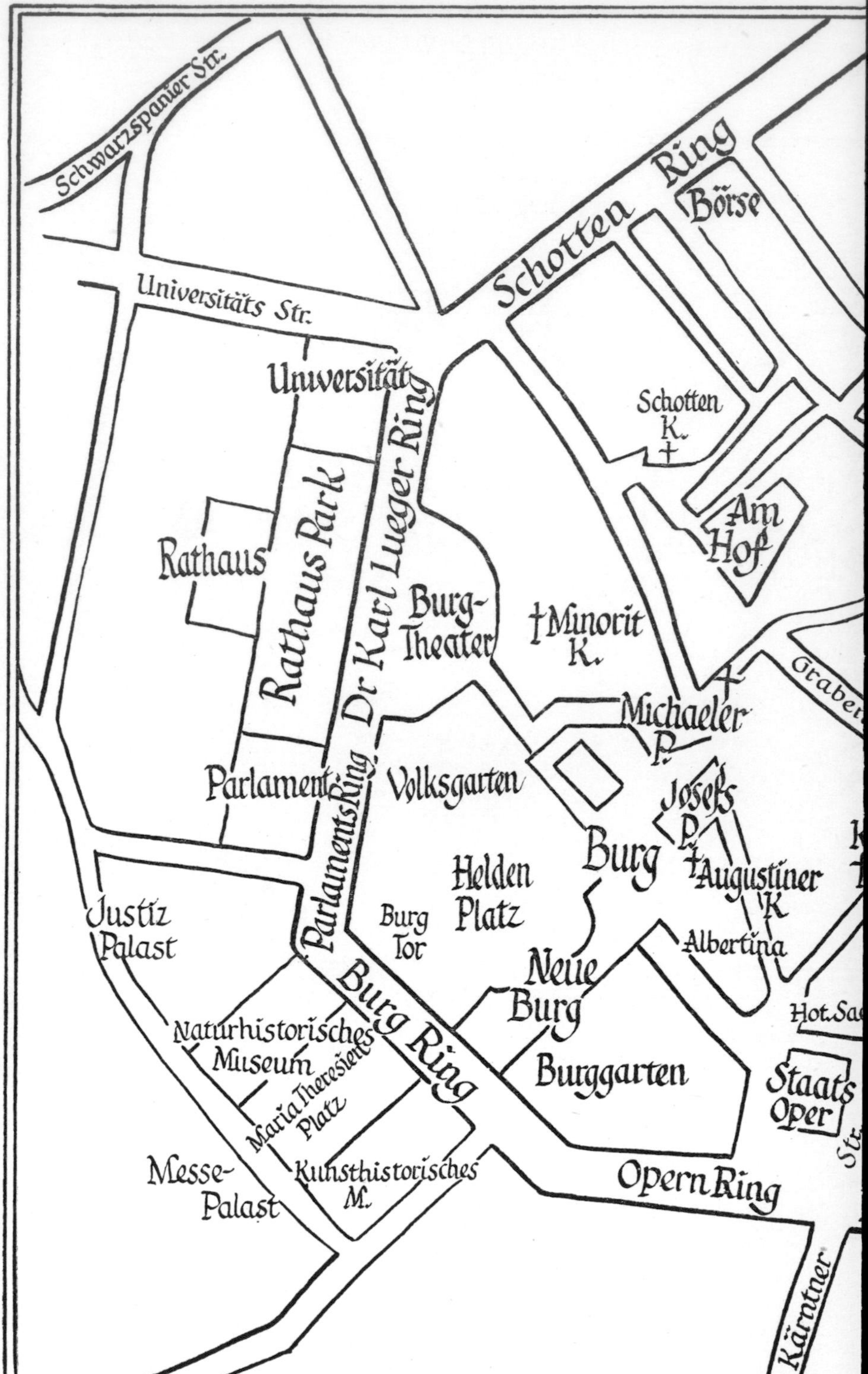

Schwarzspanier Str.

Schotten Ring

Börse

Universitäts Str.

Universität

Schotten K. †

Dr Karl Lueger Ring

Rathaus Park

Rathaus

Am Hof

Burg-Theater

† Minorit K.

Michaeler P. †

Grabe

Parlamentsring

Parlament

Volksgarten

Burg

Josefs P. †

† Augustiner K.

Helden Platz

Justiz Palast

Burg Tor

Albertina

Neue Burg

Hot. Sac

Naturhistorisches Museum

Burg Ring

Maria Theresien Platz

Burggarten

Staats Oper

Str.

Messe-Palast

Kunsthistorisches M.

Opern Ring

Kärntner Str.

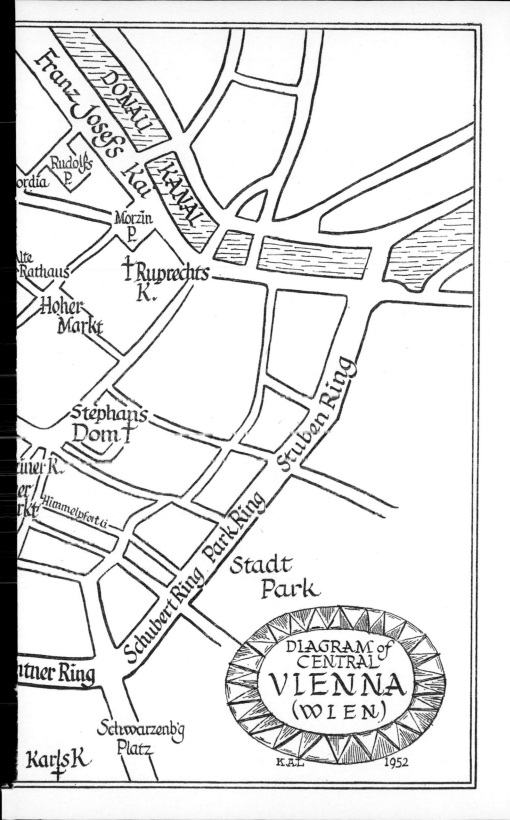

INDEX

The numerals in **heavy type** *refer to the* **figure numbers** *of the illustrations.*

255